SPANISH FOR PROFESSIONALS IN RADIOLOGY

An English/Spanish Pocket Guide

By Olive Peart

Translated in part by
Lizette Padilla
& Edwin Resto

For further information, contact:
Peltrovijan Publishing P.O. Box 13, Shrub Oak NY 10588-1801
E-mail: peltrovijan@yahoo.com. Fax:914-962-0767
Online: http://www. peltrovijan.com ISBN:1-889534-12-9

CONTENTS

HOW TO BEST UTILIZE THIS BOOK

This book was not designed to teach the Spanish language. However, ***SPANISH FOR PROFESSIONALS*** IN RADIOLOGY can easily be used by someone with a limited knowledge of Spanish.

The main purpose of the book is to communicate your instructions to the patient and to understand everyday emergency situations the Spanish patient may present. The Spanish translates simple everyday phrases a technologist uses and can also enable you to help the Spanish patient who is seeking information or directions.

The emphasis is on being understood and not necessarily on achieving an authentic Spanish accent. Most of the Spanish used is followed by a phonetic transcription, syllable by syllable, showing you how to pronounce the words. The bold letters in the transcription indicate the stressed syllables. The transcription is based on the Latin American pronunciation, and should be read just as one would read ordinary English. Please also note that although the transcription is divided into syllables, spoken Spanish is a fast and fluid language. You should pronounce the stressed syllables louder but try to keep the stressed and unstressed syllables the same length, pronouncing each group of syllables as one word.

The Spanish in this book includes the technical terms used in hospitals and clinics, and most of the phrases and expressions are simple and easy to remember.

While it is not necessary to memorize the entire book, if you are really interested in learning to communicate with your patients, it's essential that you at least read through the last eleven chapters to familiarize yourself with the language and to practice your pronunciation; you would then be able to pick out a few useful phrases to memorize. After that, you can always keep the book in your pocket for a quick reference when needed.

For those interested in learning more about the language, the chapter on Spanish grammar is brief and gives you the essentials of the language.

Olive Peart, B.S.,R.T.(R)(M))

SPANISH PRONUNCIATION

There are 5 distinct vowels in Spanish

a	as in APPLE
e	as in MET
i	similar to the English "ee" as in BEE
o	as in NO
u	similar to the English "oo" as in BOOT

The consonants are very similar to the English except for the following major changes.

b,v	both are pronounced "b" as in BOOK
c	before an -e or -i pronounced "s" as in SO otherwise it is pronounced "k" as in KING
h	the -h- in Spanish is never pronounced
j	always pronounced as "h"
ll	pronounced "y" as in YES
ñ	pronounced as "ny" as in CANYON
qu	pronounced "k" as in KING
r	the -r- in Spanish is rolled
y	pronounced "j" as in JOY - by it self or in front of a vowel pronounced "ee" as BEE
z	pronounced "s" as in SO

Also remember:

In Spanish the next-to-last syllable of words ending in a vowel, -n or -s is always stressed. The last syllable of words ending in a consonant (except the -n or -s) is stressed. All words that do not follow these rules have a written accent.

SPANISH GRAMMAR IN BRIEF

NOUNS

All nouns in Spanish are either masculine or feminine.

Masculine nouns generally end with "o" or are names that are naturally masculine. *eg. el hombre: the man.*

Days of the week, months, rivers, oceans, and mountains are also masculine.

Feminine nouns generally end with "a" and are also nouns that are naturally feminine. *eg. la mujer: the woman.*

In most cases to change a word from masculine to feminine simply change the ending of the word from "o" to "a".
eg. el niño: the boy; la niña: the girl.

For masculine nouns ending in "ón," "or" or "án," add an "a" for the feminine. *eg. el doctor: la doctora*

ARTICLES

The articles in Spanish agree with the nouns in gender and number.

	singular	**plural**
mas.	the/a boy: el/un niño	the boys : los niños
		boys : unos niños
fem.	the/a girl: la/una niña	the girls : las niñas
		girls : unas niñas

Definite articles are used instead of possessive adjectives for objects close to the body and for body parts.
eg. levante las manos: lift your hands.

PRONOUNS

Personal Pronouns

I	*yo*
you	*tú* - used to address relatives, close friends or children
you	*usted* - the polite form used to address strangers
he/she/it	*él/ella*
we	*nosotros/nosotras*
you(pl.)	*ustedes* - polite form
they	*ellos/ellas*

Pronouns in front of the verb are frequently omitted in Spanish except in the polite form (usted, ustedes).
eg. Yo hablo español becomes *Hablo español.*

Direct Object Pronouns

Direct object pronouns are used instead of direct objects.

me	*me*
you	*te*
you	*lo* (polite form)
him/her/it	*lo/la*
us	*nos*
you(pl.)	*los* (polite form)
them	*los/las*

Direct object pronouns are placed before a conjugated verb.
eg. *¿Dónde le duele?:* Where does it hurt?

Indirect Object Pronouns

An indirect object usually tells to whom or for whom something is done.

to me	*me*
to you	*te*
to you	*le*
to him/her	*le*
to us	nos
to you(pl.)	*les* (polite form)
to them	*les*

The indirect object pronoun is usually placed in front of the verb. When used with an infinitive, it can be attached to the infinitive, forming one word. *eg. ¿En qué puedo ayudarle?* : Can I help you?

Possessive Pronouns

Possessive pronouns agree in gender and number with the person or thing possessed and are generally used with the definite articles. *(el, la, los & las)*

The exception is with the verb "ser": to be.
eg. They are mine. : *Son mías.* - not - *Son las mías.*

	Singular		Plural	
	Mas.(el)	**Fem.(la)**	**Mas.(los)**	**Fem.(las)**
mine	*mío*	*mía*	*míos*	*mías*
yours	*tuyo*	*tuya*	*tuyos*	*tuyas*
yours *(polite)* *his, hers*	*suyo*	*suya*	*suyos*	*suyas*
ours	*nuestro*	*nuestra*	*nuestros*	*nuetras*
theirs	*suyo*	*suya*	*suyos*	*suyas*

Reflexive Pronouns

In English the reflexive pronoun is often understood but not used.

	subject	**reflexive pronoun**
myself, to(for)myself	yo	me
yourself, to(for) yourself	tú	te
yourself, to(for) yourself	usted	se
himself,herself,itself to(for) himself, herself itself	él/ella	se
ourselves, to(for) ourselves	nosotros	nos
yourselves, to(for) yourselves (formal)	ustedes	se
themselves, to(for) themselves	ellos/ellas	se

Reflexive pronouns are placed before the verb in the sentence.
eg. El paciente se viste : The patient dresses himself.

Demonstrative Pronouns

	Mas.	**Fem.**	**Neuter**
this	éste	ésta	esto
these	éstos	éstas	estos
that	ése	ésa	eso
those	ésos	ésas	esos
that (one)	aquél	aquélla	aquello
those (at a distance)	aquéllos	aquéllas	aquellos

The neuter pronouns can be used to refer to situations or ideas. All the demonstrative pronouns have a written accent to differentiate them from the demonstrative adjectives. The exceptions are the neuter pronouns. They have no accent marks because there are no corresponding demonstrative adjectives.

ADJECTIVES

Demonstrative Adjectives

Demonstrative adjectives point out persons and things. They agree in gender and number with the nouns they modify. The forms of the demonstrative adjectives are the same as those of the demonstrative pronouns except that the demonstrative adjectives do not have a written accent.

Possessive Adjectives

Possessive adjectives agree in number with the nouns they modify (that is, what is possessed).

	Sing.	**Plur.**
my	*mi*	*mis*
your	*tu*	*tus*
your(polite)	*su*	*sus*
his/hers/it	*su*	*sus*
our	*nuestro/a*	*nuestros/as*
their	*su*	*sus*

Nuestros is the only possessive adjective that agrees in number AND IN GENDER with what is possessed.

eg. *nuestro hijo* our son
nuestra hija our daughter
nuestros hijos our sons
nuestras hijas our daughters

In general adjectives in Spanish agree in gender and number with the noun. Qualifying adjectives (good, color, etc.) generally follow nouns, while adjectives of quantity (four, many, etc.) precede them.

eg. *el libro azul* the blue book
los libros azules the blue books
cuatro libros four books

Also: Adjectives ending in "o" change to "a" for the feminine form. Adjectives ending in "e" or a consonant have the same masculine and feminine forms. The exception to this is any adjective of nationality ending in a consonant in which case an "a" is added in the feminine.

eg. *el niño español* the spanish boy
la niña española the spanish girl

COMPARATIVE AND SUPERLATIVE

In Spanish, apart from a few irregular forms, the comparative is formed by adding "más que" (more than) or "menos que" (less than) before the adjective or adverb.

eg. La enfermera es más alta que tu. : The nurse is taller than you.

Superlatives are formed by placing the definite article (el or la) before the person or thing being compared.

eg. La enfermera más alta. : The tallest nurse.

ADVERBS

Adverbs, which are formed in the English language by adding "ly" to the adjective form of the word, are formed in the Spanish language by adding "mente" to the feminine form of the adjective. For adjectives ending in "o" change the "o" to "a" before adding "mente."

eg. *lento* : slow *lentamente* : slowly
rápido : rapid *rápidamente* : rapidly

If two or more adjectives are used together change the "o" to "a" in both but end only the last one with "mente."

eg. slowly and carefully : *lenta y cuidadosamente*

"ING" ENDINGS

The verbal endings "ando" and "iendo" translate to the English ending "ing." In Spanish the verb to be ,"estar" is used with the past participle.

eg. Estoy escribiendo I am writing
¿Está usted usando....? Are you wearing....?

TO SHOW POSSESSION

Instead of the apostrophe Spanish uses the word "de."

eg. La requisición de paciente : The patient's requisition
La radiografía de la niña : The girl's x-ray

DIRECT COMMANDS

When giving a direct affirmative command, the object pronouns are placed after the verb and are attached to it, forming one word. In the negative command the object pronouns are placed in front of the verb.

eg. ¡Escribalo aquí! Write that down here!
¡No los ponga aquí! Do not put them here!

Note that negatives in Spanish are formed simply by putting -no- in front of the verb. *eg. ¡No toque aqui!* : Do not touch here!

VERBS

Reflexive Verbs

Most verbs can be made reflexive in Spanish by adding the reflexive pronoun. Reflexive verbs act upon the subject.

Regular Verbs

There are three main catagories of regular verbs in Spanish: those ending in either "ar," "er" or "ir." The other Spanish verbs are irregular verbs and their conjugations have to be learned. Below are the conjugations in the present tense of the verbs "ser" and "estar."

There are two verbs in Spanish for "to be": "Ser" used to describe a permanent condition and "Estar" used to describe a temporary condition.

		SER	ESTAR
yo	I am	soy	estoy
usted	you are	es	está
el(ella)	her/she/it is	es	está
nosotros/as	we are	somos	estamos
ustedes	you are	son	están
ellos(ellas)	they are	son	están

WORDS THAT HAVE THE SAME SPELLING BUT DIFFERENT MEANINGS

el	the	*él*	he,him
mas	but	*más*	more
mi	my	*mí*	me
si	if	*sí*	yes
te	you	*té*	tea
tu	your	*tú*	you

Also: éste - this

With the accent it is used as a pronoun, but without the accent it is an adjective or it can be a noun.

eg. el este : the east

And: *ésta* - this

Like "este" this word is a pronoun with the accent and an adjective without the accent. "Está" is also the conjugated form of the verb "estar" to be.

eg. usted está : you are
el/ella está : he/she/it is

REFERENCES

Numbers/ Months/ Seasons/ Days & Dates/ Time/ Color and Clothing/ Bones of the Body.

Numbers

0	*cero*	SEH-roh
1	*uno*	OOnoh
2	*dos*	dos
3	*tres*	trehs
4	*cuatro*	KWAH-troh
5	*cinco*	SEEN-koh
6	*seis*	sehss
7	*siete*	SEE-EHteh
8	*ocho*	OH-choh
9	*nueve*	NWEH-beh
10	*diez*	dee-es
11	*once*	ON-seh
12	*doce*	DOH-seh
13	*trece*	TREH-seh
14	*catorce*	kah-TORseh
15	*quince*	KEEN-seh
16	*dieciséis*	dee-see-SEHES
17	*diecisiete*	dee-see-SEE-EHteh
18	*dieciocho*	dee-see-OH-choh
19	*diecinueve*	dee-see-NWEH-beh
20	*veinte*	BEHNteh
21	*veintiuno*	behn-teeOOnoh
22	*veintidos*	behn-teeDOS
23	*veintitrés*	behn-teeTREHS
24	*veinticuatro*	behn-teeKWAH-troh
25	*veinticinco*	behn-teeSEEN-choh
26	*veintiséis*	behn-teeSEHSS
27	*veintisiete*	behn-teeSEE-EHteh
28	*veintiocho*	behn-teeOH-choh
29	*veintinueve*	behn-teeNWEH-beh
30	*treinta*	TREHNtah
31	*treinta y uno*	TREHNtah ee OOnoh
32	*treinta y dos*	TREHNtah ee dos
33	*treinta y tres*	TREHNtah ee trehs
40	*cuarenta*	kwah-REHNtah
41	*cuarenta y uno*	kwah-REHNtah ee OOnoh
50	*cincuenta*	seen-KWENtah

51	*cincuenta y uno*	seen-KWENtah ee OOnoh
60	*sesenta*	seh-SEHNtah
61	*sesenta y uno*	seh-SEHNtah ee OOnoh
70	*setenta*	seh-TEHNtah
71	*setenta y uno*	seh-TEHNtah ee OOnoh
80	*ochenta*	oh-CHEHNtah
81	*ochenta y unooh*	CHEHNtah ee OOnoh
90	*noventa*	noh-BEHNtah
91	*noventa y uno*	noh-BEHNtah ee OOnoh
100	*cien*	see-en
101	*ciento uno*	SEE-ENtoh OOnoh
110	*ciento diez*	SEE-ENtoh dee-es
120	*ciento veinte*	SEE-ENtoh BEHN-teh
200	*doscientos*	dosSEE-ENtos
300	*trescientos*	trehsSEE-ENtos
400	*cuatrocientos*	kwahtroSEE-ENtos
500	*quinientos*	keeNEE-ENtos
600	*seiscientos*	sehssSEE-ENtos
700	*setecientos*	seh-tehSEE-ENtos
800	*ochocientos*	oh-chohSEE-ENtos
900	*novecientos*	noh-behSEE-ENtos
1,000	*mil*	meel
1,100	*mil cien*	meel see-en
1,600	*mil seiscientos*	meel sehssSEE-ENtos
2,000	*dos mil*	dos meel
10,000	*diez mil*	dee-es meel
100,000	*cien mil*	see-en meel
1,000,000	*un millon*	oon meejon

Ordinal Numbers

first	*primero*	preeMEH-roh
second	*segundo*	sehGOON-doh
third	*tercero*	terSEH-roh
fourth	*cuarto*	KWAR-toh
fifth	*quinto*	KEENtoh
sixth	*sexto*	SEKS-toh
seventh	*séptimo*	SEPtee-moh
eighth	*octavo*	ohkTAH-boh
ninth	*noveno*	nobEH-noh
tenth	*decimo*	DEHsee-moh
once	*una vez*	OOnah bes

twice	*dos veces*	dos BEHses
three times	*tres veces*	trehs BEHses
a half	*una mitad*	OOnah meeTAD
half of...	*la mital de...*	lah meeTAD deh...
one third	*un tercio*	oon TEHRsee-oh
5.2%	*cinco, dos ciento*	SEENkoh (KOHmah) dos SEE-ENtoh

MONTHS

January	*enero*	eh-NEHroh
February	*febrero*	feh-BREHroh
March	*marzo*	MAR-soh
April	*abril*	ah-BREEL
May	*mayo*	MAH-joh
June	*junio*	HOOnee-oh
July	*julio*	HOOlee-oh
August	*agosto*	ah-GOHStoh
September	*septiembre*	sep-TEE-EMbreh
October	*octubre*	ok-TOObreh
November	*noviembre*	noh-BEE-EMbreh
December	*diciembre*	dee-SEE-EMbreh

The months of the year, the days of the week and the seasons, are not capitalized in Spanish.

SEASONS

spring	*la primavera*	lah pree-mah-BEHrah
summer	*el verano*	el beh-RAHnoh
autumn	*el otoño*	el oh-TOHnyoh
winter	*el invierno*	el eenBEERnoh

DAYS & DATES

Monday	*lunes*	LOO-nehs
Tuesday	*martes*	MAR-tehs
Wednesday	*miércoles*	MEERkoh-les
Thursday	*jueves*	HWEH-bes
Friday	*viernes*	BEE-ERnes
Saturday	*sábado*	SAHbah-doh
Sunday	*domingo*	doh-MEENgoh

What is today's date?	*¿Qué fecha es hoy?* keh FEH-chah es oi
Today is Monday.	*Hoy es lunes.* oi es LOO-nes
It is the1st of January.	*Hoy es el primero de enero* * oi es el pree-MEHroh de eh-NEHroh
on Tuesday	*el martes* el MAR-tes
last week	*la semana pasada* lah seh-MAHnah pah SAHdah
the day before	*el día anterior* el DEE-ah an-tehREE-OR
yesterday	*ayer* ah-JER
yesterday morning	*ayer por la mañana* ah-JER pohr lah mah-NYAHnah
yesterday afternoon	*ayer por la tarde* ah-JER pohr lah TAR-deh
last night	*la noche pasada* lah NOH-cheh pah-SAHdah
the day before yesterday	*anteayer* an-teh-ahJER
two days ago	*hace dos días* AH-seh dos DEE-as
today	*hoy* oi
during the day	*durante el día* dooRANteh el DEE-ah
this morning	*esta mañana* ES-tah mah-NYAHnah
this afternoon	*esta tarde* ES-tah TAR-deh

tonight	*esta noche* ES-tah NOH-cheh
tomorrow	*mañana* mah-NYAHnah
tomorrow evening	*mañana por la tarte* mah-NYAHnah pohr lah TAR-deh
tomorrow night	*mañana por la noche* mah-NYAHnah pohr lah NOH-cheh
the day after tomorrow	*pasado mañana* pah-SAHdoh mah-NYAHnah
the next day	*el día siguiente* el DEE-ah seeGIH-ENteh
in 3 days time	*en tres días* en trehs DEE-as
in 2 days time	*en dos días* en dos DEE-as
last Wednesday/month	*el miércoles/mes pasado* el MEERkoh-les/mes pah-SAHdoh
next week/month	*la semana/el mes próxima* lah seh-MAHnah/ el mes PROK-seemah
before Thursday /February	*antes de jueves/febrero* AN-tehs deh HWEH-bes/ feb-BREHroh
in March	*en marzo* en MAR-soh
since April	*desde abril* DEHS-deh ah-BREEL
not until May	*no hasta mayo* noh AS-tah MAH-joh
during June	*durante junio*doo RAN-teh HOOnee-oh

after July	*después de julio* dehs-POOES deh HOOlee-oh
the beginning of August	*principios de agosto* preen-SEEpeeos deh ah-GOHStoh
the middle of September	*mediados de septiembre* meh-DEEah-dos deh sep-TEE-EMbreh
the end of October	*finales de octubre* feen-AHles deh ok-TOObreh
this year	*este año* ES-teh AH-nyo
last year	*el año pasado* el AH-nyoh pah-SAHdoh
next year	*el año proximo* el AH-nyos PROKsee-moh
in 1990	*en mil novecientos noventa* en meel noh-behSEE-ENtos noh-BEHNtah
1992	mil novecientos noventa y dos meel noh-behSEE-ENtos noh-BEHNtah ee dos

* The ordinal number -primero- is used when refering to the first day of the month.

TIME

What time is it?	*¿Que hora es?* keh oh-rah es
It is....	*Es... or Son...* es / sohn
...one o'clock.	*...la una.* lah oona
...eight o'clock.	*...las ocho.* las OH-choh
...eight fifteen.	*...las ocho y cuarto.* las OH-choh ee KWAR-toh

...eight twenty.	*...las ocho y veinte.* las OH-choh ee BEHNteh
...eight thirty.	*...las ocho y media.* las OH-choh ee MEH-deeah
...eight fortyfive.	*...las nueve menos cuarto.* las NWEH-beh MEH-nos KWAR-toh
...nine o'clock.	*...las nueve.* las NWEH-beh
...nine ten.	*...las nueve y diez.* las NWEH-beh ee dee-es
...nine forty	*...las diez menos veinte.* las dee-es MEH-nos BEHN-teh

Note that "es" is always used with "una" and "son" with all the other hours. Also, the hour is always said before the minutes and is always given a definite article.

at one o'clock	*a la una* ah lah oona
at four p.m.	*a las cuatro de la tarde* ah las KWAH-troh deh lah tar-deh
in the morning	*por la mañana* pohr lah mah-NYAHnah
in the afternoon	*por la tarde* pohr lah TAR-deh
at night	*por la noche* pohr lah NOH-cheh
in ten minutes	*en diez minutos* en dee-es mee-NOOtos
in 1/4 of an hour	*en un cuarto de hora* en oon KWAR-toh deh oh-rah
in 1/2 an hour	*en media hora* en meh-DEEah oh-rah
in 3/4 of an hour	*en tres cuartos de hora* en trehs KWAR-tos deh oh-rah

COLOR AND CLOTHING

Color

black	*negro*	NEH-groh
blue	*azul*	ah-SOOL
brown	*marrón, café*	mah-RON, cah-FEH
green	*verde*	BER-deh

grey	*gris*	grees
orange	*naranja, anaranjado*	nah-RANhah, ah-nahran-HAHdoh
pink	*rosado*	roh-SAHdoh
purple	*purpúra*	poor-POOrah
red	*rojo*	ROH-hoh
silver	*de plata, plateado*	deh PLAH-tah, plah-tehAHdoh
white	*blanco*	BLAN-koh
yellow	*amarillo*	ah-mahREEjoh
light	*claro*	KLAH-roh
dark	*oscuro*	os-KOOroh
corduroy	*pana*	PAH-nah
cotton	*algodón*	al-gohDON
leather	*cuero*	KWEH-roh
silk	*seda*	SEH-deh
wool	*lana*	LAH-nah
artificial	*artificial*	ar-tee-feeSEE-AL
synthetic	*sintético*	seen-TEHtee-coh

Clothing

bag	*la cartera*	kahr-TEHrah
belt	*la correa, la cinto*	kohREH-ah, SEEN-toh
blouse	*la blusa, la camisa*	BLOO-sah, kahMEE-sah
boot	*la bota*	BOH-tah
bra	*el sostén*	sohs-TEN
bracelet	*la pulsera*	poolSEH-rah
cap	*el/la gorro/a*	GOH-roh/ah
chains	*las cadenas*	kahDEH-nas
clothes	*la ropa*	ROH-pah
coat	*la capa*	KAH-pah
dress	*el vestido*	besTEE-doh
dressing gown	*la bata*	BAH-tah
earrings	*los pantallas*	panTAH-jas
glove	*el guante*	GWAN-teh
hairpin/clip	*la pinche de pelo*	PEEN-cheh deh PEH-loh
hat	*el sombrero, el gorro*	somBREH-roh, GOH-roh

jacket	*el chaqueta*	jah-KEHtah
jeans	*los vaqueros*	bah-KEHros
jewelry	*la joyería*	hoh-jehREE-ah
	la prenda	PREN-dah
necklace	*el collar*	koh-JAHR
nightdress/ clothing	*el camisón*	kah-meeSON
panties	*las bragas*	BRAH-gas
pants	*los pantalones*	pan-tah-LOHnes
panty-hose	*la media pantalón*	meh-DEEah pan-tahLON
raincoat	*la capa*	KAH-pah
	el impermeable	eem-per-mehAH-bleh
ring	*la sortija*	sorTEE-hah
sandal	*la chancleta*	chan-KLEHtah
	la zapatilla	sah-pahTEE-jah
shirt	*la camiseta*	kah-meeSEH-tah
	la camisa	kah-MEEsah
shoe	*el zapato*	sah-PAHtoh
shorts	*los calzoncillos*	kal-sohnSEEjos
skirt	*la falda*	FAL-dah
sock/ stocking	*la media*	meh-DEEah
slipper	*la chancleta*	chan-KLEHtah
sneaker	*la tenis*	TEH-nees
stocking	*la pantaleta*	pan-tahLEH-tah
sweater	*el suéer*	SWEH-ter
tie	*la corbata*	kor-BAHtah
undershirt	*la camiseta*	kah-meeSEHtah
underwear	*la ropa interior*	ROH-pah een-TEHReeor
wrist- watch	*el reloj de pulsera*	reh-LOH deh pool-SEHRrah
zipper	*el zipper, la cremallera*	see-PER kreh-mah-JERrah

BONES & BODY PARTS

abdomen	*el abdomen*	ab-DOHmen
ankle	*el tobillo*	toh-BEEjoh
anus	*el ano*	AH-noh
arm	*el brazo*	BRAH-soh
artery	*la arteria*	ar-tehREE-ah

back	*la espalda*	es-PALdah
breast	*el seno*	SEH-noh
bladder	*la vejiga*	beh-HEEgah
blood vessels	*el vasos sanguíneos*	BAH-sos san-GIHneh-os
bone	*el hueso*	oo-EHsoh
body	*el cuerpo*	KWER-poh
bowels	*los intestinos*	een-tesTEEnos
cervical spine	*la espina cervicales*	es-PEEnah ser-bee-KAHles
cheek	*la mejilla*	meh-HEEjah
chest	*el pecho*	PEH-choh
chin	*la quijada*	kee-HAHdah
clavicle	*la clavícula*	klah-BEEkoo-lah
coccyx	*el coccis*	KOK-sees
coccyx bone	*el hueso coxal*	oo-EHsoh koks-AL
colon	*el colon*	KOH-lon
diaphragm	*el diafragma*	deeah-FRAGmah
ear	*el oído*	oh-EEdoh
elbow	*el codo*	KOH-doh
esophagus	*el esófago*	eh-SOHfah-goh
eye	*el ojo*	OH-hoh
face	*la cara*	KAH-rah
femur	*el femur*	feh-MOOR
fibula	*la fíbula*	FEEboo-lah
fingers	*el/los dedo/s de la mana*	DEH-doh/os... MAH-nah
foot	*el pie*	PEE-eh
forearm	*el antebrazo*	an-teh-BRAHsoh
forehead	*la frente*	FREN-teh
gall bladder	*vesicula biliar*	behSEE-koo-lah bee-leeAR
gland	*la glandula*	glan-DOOlah
groin	*ingúinal area*	een-GIHnal ah-REEah
hair	*el pelo*	PEH-loh
hand	*la mano*	MAH-noh
head	*la cabeza*	kah-BEEsah
heart	*el corazón*	koh-rahSON
heel	*el talón*	tah-LON

hip	*la cadera*	kah-DEHrah
intestine	*el intestino*	een-tes-TEEnoh
jaws	*la mandibula*	man-dee-BOOlah
joint	*la articulación*	ar-tee-koo-lahSEEON
kidney	*el/los riñón/es*	ree-NYON/es
knee	*la rodilla*	ro-DEEjah
large bowels	*el intestino grueso*	... GRWEH-soh
leg	*la pierna*	PEE-ERnah
lip	*la labio*	lah-BEEoh
liver	*el hígado*	EEgah-doh
lower arm	*parte de abajo del brazo*	PAR-teh...ah-BAHhoh ... BRAH-soh
lumbar spine	*la espina lumbar*	... loom-BAR
lungs	*el/los pulmon/es*	pool-MOHN/es
mandible	*la mandíbula*	man-DEEboo-lah
mastoids	*la mastoide*	mas-TOYdeh
mastoid bone	*el hueso mastoideo*	... mas-TOYdee-oh
maxilla	*el/los maxila/res*	maks-EElah/res maxilla
bone	*el hueso maxilar*	... maks-EElar
mouth	*la boca*	BOH-kah
muscle	*el músculo*	MOOSkoo-loh
nasal bone	*el hueso nasal*	... nah-SAL
neck	*el cuello* / la nuca	KWEH-joh / noo-cah
nerve	*el nervio*	ner-BEEoh
nervous system	*el sistema nervioso*	seesTEHmah ner-beeOH-soh
nose	*la naríz*	nah-REES
orbits	*las orbitas*	ORbee-tah
paranasal sinuses	*los senos paranasales*	*SEH-nos* pah-rah-nah-SAHles
ethmoid	*etmoidales*	et-moy-DAHles
sphenoid	*esfenoidales*	es-feh-noy-DAHles
frontal	*frontales*	fron-TAHles
maxillary	*maxilares*	mahks-ee-LARes

pelvis	*la pelvis*	PEL-bees
pelvis bones	*los huesos pelvico*	… PELbees-koh
penis	*el pene*	PEH-neh
ribs	*las costillas*	kos-TEEjas
shoulder	*el hombro*	OHM-broh
sinuses	*los senos*	SEH-nos
skin	*la piel*	pee-EL
skull	*el cráneo*	CRAHneh-oh
small bowels	*el intestino delgado*	… del-GAHdoh
spine	*la espina*	es-PEEnah
stomach	*estómago*	es-TOHmah-goh
sole (of feet)	*la planta (del pie)*	PLAN-tah … PEE-eh
sacrum	*el sacro*	SAK-roh
sacrum bone	*el hueso sacral*	… SAK-cral
tendon	*el tendon*	TEN-dohn
thigh	*el muslo*	MOOS-loh
thoracic spine	*la espina torácica*	… toh-RAHsee-kah
throat	*la garganta*	gar-GANtah
thumb	*el dedo pulgar*	DEH-doh pool-GAR
tibia	*la tibia*	tee-BEEah
toe	*el dedo del pie*	DEH-doh ….PEE-eh
tongue	*la lengua*	LEHN-gwah
tonsils	*las tonsilos*	ton-SEElos
upper arm	*parte de arriba del brazo*	… ah-REEbah … BRAH-soh
upper leg	*parte superior de la pierna*	PAR-teh soo-peh-REEor … PEE-ERnah
ureter	*el uréter*	oo-REHter
vein	*la vena*	BEH-nah
vagina	*la vagina*	bah-GEEnah
waist	*la cintura*	seen-TOOrah
wrist	*la muñeca*	moo-NYEHkah

GENERAL GREETINGS

Hello	*Hola* OH-lah
Good morning	*Buenos dias* BWEN-os DEE-as
Good afternoon	*Buenas tardes* BWEN-as TAR-des
Good night	*Buenas noches* BWEN-as NOH-chehs
Goodbye/See you later	*Adiós /Hasta luego* Ah-deeOOS / AS-tah LWEH-goh
Yes/No	*Sí/No* See/noh
Thank you	*Gracias* GRAHsee-as
You're welcome.	*De nada /Está bien.* deh NAH-dah / es-TAH beeEN
Please	*Por favor* Pohr fah-BOHR
Yes/No... Thank you	*Sí/No... Gracias* See/noh...GRAHsee-as
Yes/No... Please	*Sí/No... Por favor* See/noh...pohr fah-BOHR
Thank you very much.	*Muchas gracias.* MOO-chas GRAHsee-as

Excuse me.	*Perdóneme/Excúseme.* Per-DOHneh-meh / Eks-KOOseh-meh
I'm sorry.	*Lo siento.* Loh seeEN-toh
How are you?	*¿Cómo está usted?* KOH-moh es-TAH oosTED
Very well /Fine thanks, and you?	*Muy bien/ Muy bien gracias, ¿y usted?* mooee beeEN / mooee beeEN GRAHsee-as, ee oosTED
Doctor	*Doctor/Doctora** Doc-TOHR/doc-TOHrah
Mr.Sir/Mrs.Madam	*Señor/Señora* Seh-NYOR/seh-NYOHrah
Miss/Young lady	*Señorita* Seh-nyoh-REEtah

* *Use "o" for the masculine and "a" for the feminine.*

USEFUL QUESTIONS AND EXPRESSIONS

I do not speak Spanish.	*No hablo español.* noh AB-loh es-pah-NYOL
I do not understand Spanish.	*No comprendo español.* noh kom-PRENdoh es-pah-NYOL
I speak only a little Spanish.	*Sólo hablo un poco de español.* SOH-loh AB-loh oon POH-koh deh es-pah-NYOH
I understand.	*Comprendo /Entiendo.* kom-PRENdoh /en-teeEN-doh
I don't understand.	*No comprendo.* noh kom-PRENdoh
Do you understand?	*¿Comprende usted?* kom-PRENdeh oosTED
I will get someone to translate for you.	*Puedo buscar algún interprete para usted.* PWEH-doh boos-CAR al-GOON eenter-PREHteh PAH-rah oosTED
I will try to help you.	*Voy a tratar de ayudarle* voy ah trah-TAR deh ah-joo-DARleh
How can I help you?	*¿En qué puedo ayudarle?* en KEH PWEH-doh ah-joo-DARleh
I will be back soon.	*Regreso pronto.* reh-GREHsoh pron-toh
Please wait here.	*Por favor, espere aquí.* pohr fah-BOOR, es-PEERreh ah-KEE

Here is the receipt.	*Aquí está el recibo.* ah-KEE es-TAH el reh-SEEboh
Have you paid for this?	*¿Tuvo que pagar por esto?* TOO-boh keh pah-GAR pohr ES-toh
This test is free.	*Este estudio es gratis.* ES-teh es-TOOdee-oh es GRAH-tees
Someone will be with you shortly.	*Alguien estará con usted pronto.* AHL-giehn es-tahRAH con oosTED PRON-toh
The cashier is over there.	*La caja está allí.* lah KAH-ah es-TAH ah-JEE
Could you please...?	*¿Por favor podría usted...?* pohr fah-BOHR poh-DREEah oosTED..
...repeat that?	*...repetir eso?* ...reh-pehTEER ES-oh
...repeat that in English?	*...repita eso en inglés?* ...reh-PIHtah ES-oh en een-GLEHS
...speak more slowly?	*...hablar más despacio?* ...ab-LAR mas des-PAHseeoh
...write that down	*...escribalo aquí?* ...eskree-BAHloh ah-KEE
I know.	*Ya sé.* yah SEH
I don't know.	*No sé.* noh SEH
Please sit down...	*Por favor, siéntese* pohr fah-BOHR, seeEN-teh-seh
...here (point).	*...aquí.* ...ah-KEE
...over here.	*...acá.* ...ah-KAH

...there (point).	*...allí.* ...ah-JEE
...over there (point).	*...allá.* ...ah-JAH
One moment please...	*Un momento, por favor...* oon moh-MENtoh, pohr fah BOHR
Come in.	*Entra.* EN-trah
This one	*Éste (m), ésta (f), esto (n)#* ES-teh, ES-tah, ES-toh
That one	*Ése* ES-eh
Those (for something near)	*Ésos (m), ésas (f)#* ES-ohs, ES-ahs
Those (distant)	*Aquéllos (m), aquéllas (f)#* Ah-KEHjohs, ah-KEHjahs
How?	*¿Cómo?* KOH-moh
What?	*¿Qué?* KEH
When?	*¿Cuándo?* QWAN-doh
Where?	*¿Dónde?* DON-deh
Why?	*¿Por qué?* pohr KEH
Who?	*¿Quién?* keeEN
Which?	*¿Cuál?/¿Cuáles?* kwal/KWAH-les
Is there?/Are there?	*¿Hay?* ahee

Where are…?/What is…?	*¿Dónde están…?/¿Qué es…?* DON-deh es-TAN…?/KEH es…?
Will that be all…?	*¿Será eso todo…?* seh-RAH ES-oh TOH-doh
Is that all?	*¿Eso es todo…?* ES-oh es TOH-doh
Anything else?	*¿Algo más?* AL-goh mas
No smoking please.	*No fume, por favor.* noh FOO-meh pohr fah-BOHR
Please put out the…	*Apague……por favor* ah-PAHkeh……pohr fah-BOHR
…cigarette	*…el cigarrillo* …el seegah-REEjoh
…the cigar	*…el cigarro* …el see-GAHroh
…the pipe	*…la pipa* …lah PEE-pah
Have you got…?	*¿Cogió usted…?* koh-geeOH oosTED
…your request?	*…su requisición?* …soo reh-kee-zee-SEEON
…your receipt?	*…su recibo?* …soo reh-SEEboh
…any medical insurance?	*…seguro médico?* …see-GOOroh MEHdee-coh
…identification?	*…identificación?* …eeden-teefee-kah-SEEON
Can I have…..please?	*¿Puedo tener….por favor?* PWEH-doh teh-NEHR… pohr fah-BOHR
…the x-ray request…	*…la requisición de radiografía…* …lah reh-kee-zee- SEEON deh rah-deeoh-grah-FEEah

May I see…
your request?

¿Me deja ver… su requisición?
me DEH-hah ber… soo reh-kee-zee-SEEON

May I see…?

¿Puedo ver…?
PWEH-doh ber

You are in the wrong department.

Está en el departamento equivocado.
es-TAH en el deh-partah-MENtoh ehkee-boh-KAHdoh

Please take this…

Por favor lleve esto….
pohr fah-BOHR JEH-beh ES-toh

…to the Nuclear Medicine dept.

…al departamento de medicina nuclear.
..al deh-partah-MENtoh de meh-dee-SEEnah noo-clehAR

…to the Ultrasound dept.

…al departamento de ultrasonido.
…al deh-partah-MENtoh deh ool-trah-soh-NEEdoh

…to the M.R.I. Dept.

…al departamento de resonancia magnética.
…al deh-partah-MENtoh deh rehsoh-NAN-seeah magNEH-teekah

…to the lab

…al laboratorio
…al laboh-rah-TOHree-oh

…to the emergency room.

…a sala de emergencia
…ah SAH-lah deh eh-mer-HENsee-ah

…to your doctor.

…a su doctor
…ah soo doc-TOHR

…to the cashier.

…a la caja
…ah lah KAH-ah

Can I make you another appointment?

¿Puedo fijar otra cita?
PWEH-doh fee-HAR OHT-rah SEE-tah

I am sorry, you are late.

Lo siento, pero llegó tarde
loh seeEN-toh PEH-roh jeh-GOH TAR-deh

Your appointment has been cancelled.	*Su cita ha sido cancelada.* soo SEE-tah ah SEE-doho kan-seh-LAHdah
We tried to contact you by phone to cancel your appointment.	*Nosotros tratamos de comunicarnos con usted por el teléfono para cancelar su cita.* noh-SOtros treh-TAHmos deh kohmoonee-CARnos con oosTED pohr el tehLEH-foh-noh PAH-rah kan-sehLAR soo SEE-tah
We were unable to contact you to cancel your appointment.	*No pudimos comunicarnos con usted para cancelar su cita.* no poo-DEEmos koh-moonee-CARnos con oosTED PAH-rah kan-sehLAR soo SEE-tah
What time is your appointment?	*¿A qué hora es su cita?* ah KEH OH-rah es soo SEE-tah
On what date is your appointment?	*¿Qué fecha tiene su cita?* KEH FEH-chah teeEN-eh soo SEE-tah
These test are by appointment only.	*Estos estudios son con cita solamente.* ES-tos es-TOOdee-ohs son kon SEE-tah soh-lah-MENteh
Do you know what study you are having today?	*¿Sabe usted qué estudio tiene hoy?* SAH-beh oosTED KEH es-TOOdee-oh teeEN-eh oi
Did you drive here?	*¿Guió usted para venir acá?* gih-OH oosTED PAR-ah ben-EER ah-KAH
Did you come alone?	*¿Vino usted sólo(a)?** BEE-noh oosTED SOH-loh(ah)
Did anyone accompany you here?	*¿Alguien lo/a* acompañó para venir aca?* AHL-giehn loh/lah ah-kom-pahNYOH PAH-rah BEN-eer ah-KAH
This is	*Está es ....* ES-tah es...

...your x-ray request.	*...su orden de rayos X.* ...soo OR-den deh RAH-jos EH-kees
...your medical. insurance card	*...su tarjeta de seguro medico* *...soo tar-HEEtah deh* seh-GOOroh MEHdee-coh
...your result.	*...su resultado.* ...soo reh-sool-TAHdoh
...your x-ray.	*...su radiografía/ su placa. @* ...soo rah-deeoh-grah-FEEah / soo PLA-kah
Please take ....this	*Por favor coge ....esto* pohr fah-BOHR KOH-geh ...ES-toh
...this card.	*...esta tarjeta.* ...ES-tah tar-HEEtah
...this report.	*...esto reporte.* ...Es-toh reh-POHR-teh
The doctor will give you the results of your test...	*El doctor le dará los resultados de su estudio...* el doc-TOHR leh DAR-rah los reh-sool-TAHdos deh soo es-TOOdee-oh
...in a few days	*...en unos dias* ...en OOnos DEE-as
...in three days time	*...en tres días* ...en trehs DEE-as
...next week.	*...la semana próxima.* ...lah seh-MAHnah PROKsee-mah
...tomorrow.	*...mañana.* ...mah-NYAHnah
Call your doctor	*Llame a su doctor...* jah-meh ah soo doc-TOHR...

...in two days.	*...en dos días.* ...en dos DEE-as
...if you feel worse.	*...si se siente peor* ...see seh seeEN-teh peh-OR
...if you feel no better.	*...si no se siente mejor.* ...see noh seh seeEN-teh meh-HOR
...in the morning.	*...por la mañana.* ...pohr la mah-NYAHnah
You cannot exit from here.	*Usted no puede salir de aquí.* oosTED noh PWEH-deh sah-LEER deh ah-KEE
Please close the door.	*Por favor, cierre la puerta.* pohr fah-BOHR, see-EHReh lah PWER-tah
Do not eat or drink anything on...	*No coma ni tome nada en...* no KOH-mah nee TOH-meh NAH-dah en
... the day before your study.	*...el día antes de su estudío.* ...el DEE-ah AN-tehs deh soo es-tooDEE-oh
... the evening before your study.	*...la noche antes de su estudío.* ... lah NOH-cheh AN-tehs deh soo es-tooDEE-oh
...the day of your study	*...el día de su estudio* ...el DEE-ah deh soo es-TOOdee-oh

 # -m- masculine, -f- feminine, -n- neutral

** Use -o- for masculine and -a- for feminine*

@ The correct Spanish word is -radiografia- but -placa- is commonly used.

UNDERSTANDING YOUR PATIENT

GENERAL QUESTIONS AND EXPRESSIONS

Do you speak Spanish?	*¿Habla usted español?* AB-lah oosTED es-pah-NYOL
Does anyone here speak Spanish?	*¿Alguien aquí habla español?* AHL-giehn ah-KEE AB-lah es-pah-NYOL
I do not understand English.	*No comprendo inglés.* noh komPREN-doh een-GLEHS
Is this the emergency room?	*¿Es éste la sala de emergencia?* es ES-teh lah SAH-lah deh eh-mer-HENsee-ah
Can you help me?	*¿Me puedo ayudar?* meh PWEH-doh ah-joo-DAR
Where is…?	*¿Dónde está…?* DON-deh es-TAH
…the bathroom?	*…el baño?* …el BAH-nyoh
…the changing/dressing room?	*…el cuarto de cambiarse* …el QWAR-toh deh kam-BEEAR-seh
Where can I find …?	*¿Dónde está…?* DON-deh es-TAH
… the public telephone	*…el teléfono público?* …el tehLEH-foh-noh POOBleek-oh
How do I get to….?	*¿Para ir…* AH-rah eer

…the bathroom?	*…el baño* …el BAH-nyoh
Can I use this telephone?	*¿Puedo utilizar este teléfono?* PWEH-doh oo-tee-leeSAR ES-teh tehLEH-foh-noh
Where can I make a telephone call?	*¿Dónde puedo llamar por teléfono?* DON-deh PWEH-doh jah-MAR pohr tehLEH-foh-noh
May I speak to …?	*¿Puedo hablar con…?* PWEH-doh AB-lar con
Is…(name)… here?	*¿Es……aquí?* es……ah-KEE
I am looking for…	*Estoy buscando…* es-toy boos-KANdoh
At what time do you close/open?	*¿A qué hora cierran/abren?* ah KEH OH-rah see-EHran/ah-BREN
At what time does….open.	*¿A qué hora abren…?* ah KEH OH-rah ah-BREN…
…the x-ray dept.	*…el departmento de rayos x* …el deh-partah-MENtoh deh RAH-jos EH-kees
At what time does the doctor arrive?	*¿A qué hora llega el doctor?* ah KEH OH-rah JEH-gah el doc-TOHR
I have an appointment with…	*Tengo una cita con…* TEN-goh OOna SEE-tah kon…
Can I have an appointment…?	*¿Me puede dar una cita…?* meh PWEH-deh dar oona SEE-tah
…right now?	*…inmediatamente?* …een-mehdee-atah-MENteh
…as soon as possible?	*…tan pronto como sea posible?* …tan PRON-toh KOH-moh SEH-ah pos-EEBleh

I can't come…	*No puedo venir…* noh PWEH-doh ben-EER
…this week.	*…ésta semana.* …ES-tah seh-MAHnah
I can come …	*Puedo venir…* PWEH-doh ben-EER
…on Tuesday.	*…el martes.* …el MAR-tehs
…when you want.	*…cuando usted quiera.* …QWAN-doh oosTED kee-EERah
Please may I have…?	*Por favor ¿puedo tener…?* pohr fah-BOHR PWEH-doh teh-NEHR…
Please, where can I get…?	*Por favor, ¿dónde puedo obtener…?* pohr fah-BOHR, DON-deh PWEH-doh ob-tehNEHR
Is there….near by?	*¿Hay….cerca?* ahee….SER-kah
…a bathroom…	*…un baño…* …oon BAH-nyoh…
…a coffee shop…	*..una tienda de café…* …OOna teeEN-dah deh kah-FEH…
…a cafeteria…	*…una cafetería…* …OOna ah-feh-teh-REEah…
…an information desk…	*…una mesa de información…* …OOna MEH-sah deh een-for-mah-SEEON
How do I get out?	*¿Cómo puedo salir?* KOH-moh PWEH-doh sal-EER
How do I get…	*¿Cómo puedo llegar…* KOH-moh PWEH-doh jeh-GAHR

...to the x-ray dept?	*...al departamento de rayos x?* al deh-partah-MENtoh deh RAH-jos EH-kees
...to the pharmacy?	*...a la farmácia?* ...ah lah far-MAHseeah
...to the lab?	*...al laboratorio?* ...al lah-boh-rah-TOHree-oh
...to the first floor?	*...al primer piso?* ...al pree-MEHR PEE-soh
...to the stairs?	*...a las escaleras?* ...a las es-kah-LEHras
...to the emergency room?	*...a la sala de emergencia?* ...a lah SAH-lah deh eh-mer-HENsee-ah
...to the coffee shop?	*...a la tiendita de café?* ...a lah tee-en-DEEtah deh kah-FEH
...to the billing dept?	*...al departamento de cobro?* ...al deh-partah-MENtoh deh KOHB-roh
...to the Nuclear Medicine dept?	*...al departamento de medicina nuclear?* ...al deh-partah-MENtoh de meh-dee-SEEnah noo-clehAR
...to the Ultrasound dept?	*...al departamento de ultrasonido?* ...al deh-partah-MENtoh deh ool-trah-soh-NEEdoh
...to the M.R.I. Dept?	*...al departamento de resonancia magnética?* ...al deh-partah-MENtoh deh rehsoh-NAN-seeah magNEH-teekah
Where is...?	*¿Dónde está...?* DON-deh es-TAH

Where can I find/get...?	*¿Dónde puedo encontrar/ conseguir...?* DON-deh PWEH-doh en-kohnTRAHR/ kohn-sehGEER
Can you direct me to...?	*¿Puedo usted indicarme la dirección a...?* PWEH-doh oosTED een-dee-CARmeh lah dee-rek-SEEON ah...
Is it far from here?	*¿Está muy lejos de aquí?* es-TAH mooee LEH-hos deh ah-KEE
How do I get there?	*¿Cómo puedo llegar allí?* KOH-moh PWEH-doh JEH-gar ah-JEE
May one	*¿Se puede ....* seh PWEH-deh
...smoke here?	*...fumar un cigarrillo aquí?* ...foo-MAR oon seegah-REEjoh ah-KEE
...wait here?	*...espere aquí?* ...es-peh-REH ah-KEE
...get something to eat here?	*...buscar algo para comer aquí?* ...boos-CAR AL-goh PAH-rah kom-EHR ah-KEE
...get out this way?	*...salir por aquí?* ...sal-EER pohr ah-KEE
How much is it?	*¿Cuánto es?* QWAN-toh es
Where do I pay?	*¿Dónde pago?* DON-deh PAH-goh
Do I pay here?	*¿Tengo que pagar aquí?* TEN-goh KEH PAH-gar ah-KEE
Do you take ...	*¿Coje usted...* koh-HEH oosTED

...credit cards?	*...tarjeta de credito?* ...tar-HEHtah deh kreh-DEEtoh
...money only?	*...dinero solamente?* ...dee-NEHroh soh-lah-MENteh
Can you give me a receipt?	*¿Puede darme un recibo?* PWEH-deh DAR-meh oon reh-SEEboh
I think this is wrong.	*Creo que esto está mal.* KREH-oh KEH ES-toh es-TAH mal
May I come in?	*¿Puedo entrar?* PWEH-doh en-TRAHR
Can I have...	*¿Puedo tener...* PWEH-doh teh-NEHR
...a lead apron?	*...un delantal de plomo?* ...oon deh-lanTAL deh PLOH-m
How long will this examination take?	*¿Cuánto tiempo tomará este estudio?* KWAN-toh teeEM-poh toh-MAHrah ES-teh esTOO-deeoh
I want to leave at ...	*Yo quiero salir a...* joh kee-EERoh sal-EER ah...
...2 o'clock.	*...las dos.* ...las dohs
Can my daughter/son stay with me?	*¿Puede mi hija/o* quedars conmigo?* PWEH-deh mee EE-hah/oh keh-DARseh kohn-MEEgoh
Can my daughter come in?	*¿Puede mi hija entrar?* PWEH-doh mee EE-ha en-TRAHR
Can I return...	*¿Puedo regresar...* PWEH-doh reh-grehSAR...

…on Monday?	*…el lunes?* el LOO-nes
…tomorrow?	*…mañana?* …mah-NYAH-nah
Please may I have…?	*¿Por favor puedo tener…?* pohr fah-BOHR PWEH-doh ten-NEHR…
Please where can I get…	*Por favor, ¿dónde puedo obtener…* pohr fah-BOHR, DON-deh PWEH-doh ob-tenNEHR
…my blood pressure taken?	*…mi presión sanguínea?* …mee preh-SEEon san-GIHneh-ah
I need…	*Necesito…* neh-seh-SEEtoh
I would like…	*Quiero…* kee-EERoh

POSSIBLE ANSWERS OR DIRECTIONS

Yes, certainly	*Sí, por supuesto* see, pohr soo-poo-EStoh
Sorry	*Lo siento* loh seeEN-toh
I don't think so.	*Creo que no.* KREH-oh keh noh
I think so.	*Yo creo.* joh KREH-oh
The bathroom is occupied. at the moment.	*El baño está ocupado en el momento.* el BAH-nyoh es-TAH ohkoo-PAHdoh en el moh MENtoh
Ask at ...	*Pregunte en ...* pre-GOONteh en
...the information desk.	*...la mesa de información.* lah MEH-sah deh een-for-mah-SEEON
...the reception desk.	*...la mesa de recepción.* ...lah MEH-sah deh reh-sepSEEON
No. The public telephone is...	*No. El teléfono público está...* noh. el tehLEH-foh-noh POOBleek-oh es-TAH
...in the Emergency room.	*...en la sala de emergéncia* ...en lah SAH-lah deh eh-mer-HENsee-ah
...on the first floor.	*...en el primer piso.* ...en el pree-MEHR PEE-soh
...by the lab.	*...cerca del laboratorio.* ...SER-kah del lah-boh-rah-TOHree-oh

Make a right/left.	*Vire a la derecha/izquierda.* BEE-reh ah lah deh-REHchah/ ees-KEYEERdah
Through here/there.	*Por aquí / allá.* pohr ah-KEE /ah-JAH
Over here/there.	*Aquí /allá.* ah-KEE /ah-JAH
Straight on	*Derecho* deh-REHchoh
Make a right/left then a right/left.	*Haga una derecha/izquierda* *luego a la derecha/izquierda.* AH-gah OOna deh-REHchah/ ees-KEYEERdah LWEH-goh ah lah deh-REHchah/ees-KEYEERdah
First left/right.	*La primera a la izquierda/* *derecha.* lah pree-MEHrah ah lah ees-KEYEERdah/ deh-REHchah
Second left/ right.	*La segunda a la izquireda/* *derecha* lah seh-GOONdah ah lah ees-KEYEERdah/ deh-REHchah
Turn left/right.	*Doble a la izquierda/derecha.* DOHB-leh ah lah ees-KEYEERdah/ deh-REHchah
After you pass the…	*Después de que pase…* dehs-POOES deh KEH PAH-seh…
…the doors.	*…la puerta.* …lah PWER-tah
…elevators.	*…las ascensores.* …las as-sen-SOHres
…information desk.	*…la mesa de información.* …lah MEH-sah deh een-for-mah-SEEON
…stairs.	*…las escaleras.* …las es-kah-LEHras

At these/those doors	*En estas/aquellas puertas* en es-TAH /ah-KEHjas PWER-tas
At the stairs	*En las escaleras* en las es-kah-LEHras
At the water fountain	*En la fuente de agua* en lah foo-ENteh deh AH-gwah
It is not far/near.	*No esta lejos/cerca* noh es-TAH LEH-hos/SER-kah
It is far/near.	*Está lejos/cerca.* es-TAH LEH-hos /SER-kah
On your (the) right/left	*A la derecha/izquierda* ah lah deh-REHchah/ ees-KEYEERdah
First/last/next	*Primer/último/próximo* pree-MEHR/OOLtee-moh/ PROKsee-moh
Opposite/behind	*Enfrente/atrás* enFREN-teh/ah-TRAS
Next to/after	*Junto a/después de* JOON-toh ah/dehs-POOES deh

**Use "o" for the masculine and "a" for the feminine.*

PROBLEMS AND EMERGENCIES

GENERAL QUESTIONS AND EXPRESSIONS

I have broken...

Se me han roto....
seh meh ahn ROH-toh

...my glasses.

...los lentes.
los LEN-tehs

...my denture.

...la dentadura.
lah den-tah-DOOrah

I have lost ....

He perdido...
heh per-DEEdoh

...my contact lens.

...los lentes de contacto/ las lentillas.
los LEN-tehs deh kon-TAHKtoh/las len-TEEyas

...my handbag/pocket book.

...la cartera.
lah kar-TEHrah

...my jewelry.

...la joyeria.
lah hoh-jehREEah

...my keys.

...las llaves.
las JAH-behs

...my necklace.

...el collar.
el koh-JAHR

...my ring.

...la sortija.
lah sor-TEEhah

...my wallet.

...el monedero.
el moh-neh-DEHroh

...my watch.

...el reloj de pulsera.
el reh-LOH deh pool-SEHRrah

...my x-ray request.

...mi orden de rayos x.
mee ohr-DEHN deh RAH-jos EH-kees

I am lost.	*Me he perdido.* meh heh per-DEEdoh
I need.../I'd like...	*Necesito.../Quiero...* neh-seh-SEEtoh.../KEE-EHroh
Can I have...	*¿Puede darme...* PWEH-deh DAR-meh...
...an aspirin?	*...una aspirina?* OOna as-peer-REEnah
...a pain killer?	*...un analgésico?* oon ahnal-GEHsee-koh
...a sedative/tranquillizer?	*...un sedativo?* oon seh-dahTEE-boh
...some facial tissue?	*...papel faciál?* pah-PEHL fah-seeAL
...some toilet paper?	*...papel de excusado/papel higiénico?* pah-PEHL deh eks-kooSAH-doh/ pah-PEHL eeAYN-nee-koh
...a sanitary napkin?	*...una toalla sanitaria?* OOna toh-AHjas san-eeTAH-reeah
...some tampons?	*...unos tampones (higiénicos)?* OOnos tamPOHN-ehs (eeAYN-nee-kos)
...some water?	*...agua?* AH-gwah
Can I have an appointment...	*¿Me puede dar una cita...* meh PWEH-deh dar OOna SEEtah...
...right now?	*...inmediatamente?* een-meh-deeah-tah-MEHNteh
...tomorrow?	...mañana? mah-NYAHnah
...as soon as possible?	*...tan pronto como sea posible?* tan PRON-toh KOH-moh SEHah poh-SEEBleh

I want to leave at 2 o'clock.	*Yo quiero salir a las dos.* joh KEE-EHroh sah-LEER ah las dohs
I have been here for one hour.	*Estoy aquí hace una hora.* es-TOY ah-KEE AH-seh OOna OH-rah
At what time does the doctor leave?	*¿A qué hora se va el doctor?* ah KEH OH-rah seh vah el doc-TOHR
I am ill.	*Estoy enfermo/a.** es-TOY en-FEHRmoh/ah
My child is ill.	*Mi hijo/a está enfermo.** mee EE-hoh/hah es-TAH en-FEHRmoh
My husband/wife...	*Mi esposo/a...** mee es-pohsoh/sah
My daughter/son...	*Mi hija/o...** mee EE-hah/oh
Can you get me a doctor?	*¿Puede llamar a un doctor?* PWEH-deh jah-MAHR ah oon doc-TOHR
I need a doctor, quickly.	*Necesito un doctor, pronto.* neh-seh-SEEtoh oon doc-TOHR, PRON-toh
I am pregant.	*Estoy embarazada.* es-TOY em-bah-rah-SAHdah
I have a heart problem.	*Tengo problemas de corazón.* TEHN-goh proh-BLEMas deh koh-rahSON
I have a pain in my chest.	*Tengo un dolor en el pecho.* TEHN-goh oon doh-LOHR en el PEH-choh
I have difficulty breathing.	*Tengo dificultad respirando.* TEHN-goh dee-fee-koolTAHD rehs-pee-RAN-doh

I am allergic to…	*Soy alérgico/a* a …* soy ALEHRgee-koh/ah ah
…penicillin.	*…la penicilina.* lah peh-nee-see-LEEnah
I am …diabetic.	*Soy…diabético/a** soy…deeah-BEHtee-koh
….asthmatic.	*…asmático/a.** ahs-MAHtee-koh/ah
I have… hemorrhoids.	*Tengo… hemorroides.* TEHN-goh….ehm-moh-ROHEE-des
…rheumatism.	*…reumatismo.* reh-oo-mah-TEESmoh
…diarrhea.	*…diarrea.* dee-ah-REHah
I am in pain.	*Me duele.* meh DWEH-leh
I've had this pain for…	*He estado con este dolor…* eh es-TAHdoh kon ES-teh doh-LOHR
…one hour/one day.	*…una hora/un día.* OOna OH-rah/ oon DEEah
…two hours/two days.	*…dos horas/dos días.* dohs OHR-ahs / dos DEE-ahs
I have a pain in my…	*Tengo un dolor en el/la…* TEHN-goh oon doh-LOHR en el/lah…
It is a…sharp pain.	*Es… dolor intenso.* es doh-LOHR een-TENsoh
…a dull ache.	*…dolor sordo.* doh-LOHR SOHR-doh
…nagging pain/continuous.	*…dolor continuo.* doh-LOHR kohn-TEEnoo-oh
My chest hurts.	*El pecho me duele.* el PEH-choh meh DWEH-leh

There/here hurts.	*Allá/aquí me duele.* ah-JAH/ah-KEE meh DWEH-leh
It hurts… a lot.	*Me duele…mucho.* meh DWEH-leh ….MOO-choh
…most of the time.	*…casi todo el tiempo.* KAHsee TOH-doh el teeEM-poh
I feel…ill.	*Me siento …enfermo/a.** meh seeEN-toh ….en-FEHRmoh/ah
…faint/weak.	*…débil.* DEH-beel
…feverish.	*…febril.* feh-BREEL
…nauseous/sick.	*…náuseas.* NAWseh-ahs
…dizzy.	*…mareado/a.** mah-reh-AHdoh/ah
I am dizzy.	*Estoy mareado.* es-TOY mah-reh-AHdoh
I am going to faint.	*Me voy a desmayar.* meh boy ah des-mahJAHR
I need…	*Necesito…* neh-seh-SEEtoh
Please can I have…?	*¿Por favor podría tener…?* pohr fah-BOHR poh-DREEah ten-EHR
I would like….please.	*Me gustaría… por favor.* meh goos-tarREE-ah…pohr fah-BOHR
…something for this cold…	*…algo para el catarro…* AL-goh PAH-rah el kah-TAHroh
…something for the flu…	*…algo para gripe…* AL-goh PAH-rah GREE-peh
I am fine now.	*Me siento bien ahora.* meh seeEN-toh beeEN ah-OHrah

RELATED QUESTIONS AND REPLIES

When?	*¿Cuándo?* KWAN-doh
Where?	*¿Dónde?* DON-deh
I'm sorry, but I can't help you.	*Lo siento, pero no puedo ayudarle.* loh seeEN-TOH, PEH-roh noh PWEH-doh ah-joo-DARleh
Can I get you....some water?	*¿Le puedo dar....aqua?* leh PWEH-doh dar....AH-gwah
...something to drink?	*...algo de tomar?* ...ALgoh deh toh-MAR
...something to eat?	*...algo de comer?* ...ALgoh deh koh-MER
...some sweets?	*...algo dulce?* ...ALgoh DOOL-seh
...a chair?	*...una silla?* ...oona SEE-jah
Please lie down over here.	*Acuéstese aquí, por favor.* ah-kooES-teh-seh ah-KEE, pohr fah-BOHR
The nurse/doctor will take your blood pressure/temperature.	*La enfermera/el doctor va a tomar la presión/ la temperatura.* lah en-fehr-MEHrah /el doc-TOHR bah ah toh-MAR lah preh-SEEON/ lah tem-pehrah-TOOrah
Where does it hurt?	*¿Dónde le duele?* DON-deh leh DWEL-eh
Does it hurt here?(point)	*¿El dolor es aquí?* el doh-LOHR es ah-KEE
Are you...	*¿Está usted...* es-TAH oosTED

…taking any medicine?	*…tomando algun medicina?* …toh-MANdoh AHL-goon meh-dee-SEEnah
…pregnant?	…embarazada? …em-bahrah-SAHdah
…allergic to any medication?	*…alérgico a algún medicamento?* …ah-LERgee-koh ah ahl-GOON meh-dee-kah-MENtoh
…asthmatic?	*…asmático/a?** …as-MAHtee-koh/ah
…diabetic?	*…diabético/a?** …deeah-BEHtee-koh/ah
…on insulin?	*…en insulina?* …en een-soo-LEEnah
Please write down all medicine that you are taking.	*Por favor escriba todo medicina que está tomando.* pohr fah-BOHR es-KREEbah TOH-doh meh-dee-SEEnah keh esTAH toh-MANdoh
What medicine are you allergic to?	*¿Qué medicina es usted alérgico?* keh meh-dee-SEEnah es oosTED ah-LERgee-koh
Please write it down.	*Por favor escribalo.* pohr fah-BOHR es-kree-BAHloh
Do you take insulin?	*¿Toma usted insulina?* TOH-mah oosTED een-soo-LEEnah
Did you take your insulin?	*¿Tomó usted la insulina?* toh-MOH oosTED lah een-soo-LEEnah
Do you have a heart problem?	*¿Tiene algún problema del corazón?* teeEN-eh ahl-GOON proh-BLEMah del koh-rahSON
Take this now.	*Tome esto ahora.* TOH-meh EStoh ah-OHrah

Sit down here.	*Siéntese aquí.* see-ENteh-seh....ah-KEE
Lie down.	*Acuéstese.* *ah-KOOESteh-seh*
Breathe deeply.	*Respire profundo.* res-PEEreh pro-FOONdoh
Breathe through your mouth.	*Coja aire por la boca.* KOH-hah AY-reh pohr lah BOH-kah
Take a big breath and hold it.	*Respira profundo y aguántalo.* res-PEErah proh-FOONdoh ee ah-GWANtah-loh
Open your mouth.	*Abra la boca.* AH-brah lah BOH-kah
Cough please.	*Tosa, por favor.* TOH-sah, pohr fah-BOHR
Come with me.	*Venga conmigo.* BEN-gah kon-MEEgoh
Follow me.	*Sígame.* SEEgah-meh
Wait here.	*Espere aquí.* es-PEHreh ah-KEE
I will get a doctor.	*Yo podría conseguir al doctor.* joh poh-DREEah kon-sehGEER al doc-TOHR
You must fill this prescription today.	*(Usted) Debe conseguir esta prescripcion hoy.* (oosTED)DEH-beh konseeGEER ES-tah prehs-creep-SEEON oi
Take...teaspoons of this medicine.	*Tome...cucharillas de esta medicina.* TOH-meh...koo-chah-REEjas deh ES-tah meh-dee-SEEnah
Take this/these pills...	*Tome esta/estas píldora/s...* TOH-meh ES-tah/ES-tas PEEL-doh-rah/as

...with a glass of water.	*...con un vaso de agua.* kon oon BAH-soh deh AH-gwah
...tonight.	*...noche.* NOH-cheh
...now.	*...ahora.* ah-OHrah
...every hour.	*...cada hora.* KAH-dah OH-rah
...every...hours.	*...cada...horas.* KAH-dah...OH-ras
...twice /4 times a day.	*...dos/cuatro veces al día.* dos/KWAH-troh BEH-sehs al DEEah
...before/after each meal.	*...antes/después de cada comida.* AN-tes/deh-POOES deh KAH-dah koh-MEEdah
...in the morning/at night.	*...por la mañana/ por la noche.* pohr lah mah-NYAHnah/ pohr lah NOH-cheh
...in case of pain.	*...en caso de dolor.* en KAH-soh deh doh-LOR
...for...days.	*...durante...días.* doo-RANteh...DEE-as

* *Use "o" for the masculine and "a" for the feminine.*

FILLING OUT FORMS

GENERAL QUESTIONS AND EXPRESSIONS

What is your name?	*¿Cómo se llama?* KOH-moh seh JAH-mah
Have you had previous x-rays here?	*¿Ha tenido aquí radiografías anteriormente?* ah teh-NEEdoh ah-KEE rah-deeoh-grah-FEEas an-teh-reeohr-MEHNteh
...an Ultrasound?	*...un ultrasonido?* ... oon ool-trah-soh-NEEdoh
...an M.R.I?	*...una resonancia magnética?* ...OOnah rehsoh-NAN-seeah magNEH-teekah
When?	*¿Cuándo?* KWAN-doh
Where were your x-rays taken?	*¿En dónde le tomaron los radiografías (los placas)?#* en DON-deh leh toh-MAHron las rah-deeoh-grah-FEEas (las PLAH-kas)
What is your age?	*¿Cuál es su edad?* kwal es soo eh-DAD
Are you pregnant?	*¿Está usted embarazada?* es-TAH oosTED em-bah-rah-SAHdah
What is your...	*¿Cuál es su...* kwal es soo...
...address?	*...dirección?* dee-rek-SEEON
...name?	...nombre? NOHM-breh

...your spouse's name?	*...nombre de su esposo/a?** NOHM-breh deh soo esPOH-soh/sah
...doctor's name?	*...nombre de su doctor?* NOHM-breh deh soo doc-TOHR
...last name?	*...apellido?* ah-peh-JEEdoh
...first name?	*...primer nombre?* pree-MEHR NOHN-breh
...maiden name?	*..nombre de soltera?* NOHM-bre deh sohl-TEHrah
...place of birth?	*...lugar de nacimiento?* loo-GAHR deh nah-see-meeEN-toh
...date of birth?	*...fecha de nacimiento?* FEH-cha deh nah-see-meeEN-toh
...business number?	*...número del trabajo?* NOOmeh-roh del trah-BAHoh
...home phone number?	*...número de la casa?* NOOmeh-roh deh lah KAH-sah
...social security number?	*...número de seguro social?* NOOmeh-roh deh seh-GOOroh soh-seeAL
...business address?	*...dirección del trabajo?* dee-rek-SEEON del trah-BAHoh
...occupation?	*...ocupación?* oh-koo-pah-SEEON
...zip code?	*...zona postal?* SOHnah pohs-TAHL
...City and State?	...Ciudad y Estado? see-ooDAD ee esTAH-doh.
What is the...	*¿Cuál es el...* kwal es el

...your spouse work address?

*...direción del trabajo de su esposo/a**
dee-rek-SEEON del trah-BAHoh deh soo esPOH-soh/sah

Where do you work?

¿Dónde usted trabaja?
DON-deh oosTED trah-BAHhah

What is your health insurance number?

¿Cuál es su número de su seguro medico?
kwal es soo NOOmeh-roh deh soo seh-GOOroh MEHdee-coh

May I see your health insurance card?

¿Puedo ver su tarjeta de seguro médico?
PWEH-doh ber soo tar-HEHtah deh seh-GOOroh MEHdee-coh

Do you have...

¿Tiene usted...
teeEN-eh oosTED

...health insurance?

...seguro médica?
...seh-GOO-roh MEHdee-kah

...any children?

...hijos?
...EE-hos

How many children do you have?

¿Cuántos hijos tiene?
KWAN-tos EE-hos teeEN-eh

Are you married?

*¿Es usted casado/a?**
es oosTED kah-SAHdoh/ah

What is the name of your family doctor?

¿Cuál es el nombre de su médico de familia?
kwal es el NOHM-breh deh soo MEHdee-coh deh fahMEELeeah

Please...

Por favor...
pohr fah-BOHR...

...fill out this form.

...llene este formulario.
JEH-neh ES-teh for-moo-LAHreeoh

...sign here.

...firme aquí.
FEER-meh ah-KEE

...take this to the billing department.

...lleve esto al departamento de cobro.
JEH-beh ES-toh al deh-partah-MENtoh deh KOHB-roh

...write here.

...escríbalo aquí.
...es-KREEBAH-loh ah-KEE

...write your name here.

...escriba su nombre aquí.
...es-KREEbah soo NOHM-breh ah-KEE

RELATED REPLIES

My name is …	*Mi nombre es…/Me llamo…* mee NOHM-breh es…/meh JAH-moh…
I am …	(Yo) soy… (joh) so
…married.	*…casado/a.** …kah-SAHdoh/ah
…single.	*…soltero/a.** …sohl-TEHroh/ah
…widowed.	*…viudo/a.** …BEE-OOdoh
…divorced.	*…divorciado/a.** …dee-bor-SEE-AHdoh/ah
I have…	*(Yo) tengo…* (joh) TEHN-goh
…one daughter.	*…una hija* OOnah EE-hah
…one son.	*…un hijo.* …oon EE-hoh
…two daughters/sons.	*…dos hijas/hijos.* …dos EE-has/EE-hos
I don't have any children.	*No tengo hijos/as.* noh TEHN-goh EE-hos/as
I am pregnant.	*Estoy embarazanda.* es-TOY em-bah-rah-SAHdah
I am a student.	*Soy estudiante.* soy es-too-DEE-ANteh

**Use "o" for the masculine and "a" for the femine.*
 # Although incorrect, the word "placa" is commonly used to refer to an x-ray. The correct Spanish word is radiografía

PATIENT CONTACT

GENERAL

See the chapter on general greetings

Come this way.	*Venga acá.* BEN-gah ah-KAH

UNDRESSING THE PATIENT

The changing room is…	*El cuarto de cambiarse es…* el QWAR-toh deh cam-BEEAR-seh es…
…this way.	*…en este lado.* en ES-teh LAD-doh
…over there.	*…allá.* ah-JAH
…over here.	*…aquí.* ah-KEE
Remove your clothes please.	*Desvístase, por favor.* des-BEEStah-seh, pohr fah-BOHR
Please remove all your clothes and put this gown on.	*Por favor, quítese todo la ropa y coloquese esta bata.* pohr fah-BOHR, KEEteh-seh TOH-doh lah ROH-pah ee koh-LOHkeh-seh ES-tah BAH-tah
Put the opening…	*Colóquese la parte…* koh-LOHkeh-seh lah PAR-teh…
…to the back.	*…hacia atrás.* AH-seeah ah-TRAS
…to the front.	*…hacia el frente.* AH-seeah el FREN-teh

Undress to the waist.	*Quítese la ropa hasta la cintura.* KEEteh-seh lah ROH-pah as-tah lah sen-TOOrah
Undress…	*Quitese la ropa…* KEEteh-seh lah ROH-pah
…from the waist up.	*…de la cintura para arríba.* deh lah sen-TOOrah PAH-rah ah-REEbah
…from the waist down.	*…de la cintura para abajo.* deh lah sen-TOOrah PAH-rah ah-BAHoh
Undress…	*Desvístase…* dehs-BEEStah-seh
…here.	*…aquí.* ah-KEE
…there.	*…allá* …ah-JAH
Are you wearing…	*¿Está usted usando…* es-TAH oosTED ooSAN-doh…
…any jewelry?	*…alguna prenda?* ahl-GOONah PREN-dah
…anything with buttons?	*…algo con botones?* AHL-goh con boh-TOHnes
…anything with pins.	*…algo con pinche?* AHL-goh con PEEN-cheh
…a bra?	*…un sostén -or- brassier?* oon soos-TEN/bras-SEEey
Please remove…	*Por favor remueva…* pohr fah-BOHR reh-MOOEH-bah
…your earring.	*…las pantallas.* las pan-TAHyas
…your chains.	*…las cadenas.* las kah-DEHnas

...your hair pins/clips.	*...las pinches de pelo.* las PEEN-chez deh PEH-loh
...your ring.	*...la sortija.* lah sor-TEEhah
...your watch.	*...el reloj.* el reh-LOH
...your bracelet.	*...la pulsera.* lah pool-SEHrah
Please remove everything from your pockets.	*Por favor, remueva todo de los bolsillos.* pohr fah-BOHR reh-MOOEH-bah TOH-doh deh los bol-SEE-jos
Do you have anything in your pockets?	*¿Usted tiene algo en los bolsillos?* oosTED teeEn-eh AHL-goh en los bol-SEE-jos
Do not tie the string	*No se amarre los tirantes de la bata.* noh seh ah-MARR-reh los tee-RAHN deh lah BAH-tah
Please untie the strings of the gown.	*Por favor sueltese los tirantes de la bata.* pohr fah-BOHR swel-TEH-seh los tee-RAHN-tehs deh lah BAH-tah
Are you wearing a bra?	*¿Tiene el sostén puesto?* teeEN-eh el soos-TEN PWES-toh
Take...off.	Quítese... KEEteh-seh
...your bra...	*...el sosten...* el soos-TEN
...your shoes...	*...los zapatos...* los sah-PAHtos
Do not take off our underwear.	*No se quite la ropa interior.* noh seh KEEteh...lah ROH-pah een-TEHReeor

Take off everything except your underwear.

Quítese todo la ropa excepto la ropa interior.
KEEteh-seh TOH-doh lah ROH-pah ek-SEPtoh lah ROH-pah een-TEHReeor

Come out when you are ready.

Salga cuando está listo.
SAL-gah KWAN-doh es-TAH LEES-toh

Go to...

Vaya...
BAH-jah

Room 1.

...al cuarto número uno.
al KWAR-toh NOOmeh-roh oonoh

...the waiting room.

...a la sala de espera.
...ah lah SAL-ah deh es-PEHrah

The bathroom is occupied.

El cuarto de baño está ocupado.
el KWAR-toh deh BAH-nyoh es TAH oh-koo-PAHdoh

PRONE EXAMINATIONS

Use this (point) to get on the table.	*Use esto para subir a la mesa.* OOseh ES-toh PAH-rah soo-BEER AH LAH MEH-sah
Use the step-on stool.	*Use el escalón.* OOseh el es-kah-LON
Can you move over onto the bed?	*¿Puede moverse hacia la cama?* PWEH-deh moh-VERseh AHsee-ah lah KAH-mah
Be careful.	*Cuidado/ Tenga cuidado.* kwee-DAHdoh / TEN-gah kwee-DAHdoh
Watch your head.	*Cuidado con la cabeza.* kwee-DAHdoh con lah kah-BEHsah
Climb up...	*Súbase....* SOObah-seh
...on the table.	*...en la mesa.* ...en lah MEH-sah
Lie down.	*Acuéstese.* ah-KOOESteh-seh
Lie on ...	*Acuéstese...* ah-KOOESteh-seh...
...your back.	*...en la espalda.* ...en lah es-PALdah
...your left/right side.	*...en el lado izquierda /derecha.* ...en el LAH-doh ees-KEYEERdah /deh-REHchah
...your stomach.	*...en el estómago.* ...en el es-TOHmah-goh

...the table.

...en la mesa.
...en lah MEH-sah

Stay in the center of the table.

Quédese en el centro de la mesa.
KEHdeh-seh en el SEN-troh deh lah MEH-sah

Move to your left/right.

Más para la izquierda/derecha.
mas PAH-rah lah ees-KEYEERdah/
deh-REHchah

Move closer to me.

Más cerca de mi.
mas SER-kah deh mee

Put your feet at this end of the table.

Coloque los pies a este final de la mesa.
koh-LOHkeh los PEE-es ah ES-teh fee-NAL deh lah MEH-sah

Keep your hands above your head.

Mantenga las manos sobre la cabeza.
man-TENgah las MAH-nos SOH-breh lah kah-BEHsah

Put your hands ...

Coloca las manos...
koh-LOHkah las MAH-nos

...above your head.

...sobre la cabeza.
...SOH-breh lah cah-BEHsah

...by your side.

...a el lado.
...ah el LAH-doh

Turn on...

Colóquese...
koh-LOHkeh-seh

...your back.

...boca arriba.
BOH-kah ah-REEbah

...your side(right/left).

...el lado(derecho/izquierdo).
...el LAH-doh (deh-REHchoh/ ees-KEYEERdoh

...your stomach.

...boca abajo.
...BOH-kah ah-BAHoh

Turn...

Muévase...
MOO-EHbah-seh

...to me.

...hacia mi.
AH-seeah mee

...away from me.

...lejos de mi.
...LEH-hos deh mee

Turn over.

Voltéese.
bol-TEHeh-seh

ERECT EXAMINATIONS

Can you stand for a few minutes only?

¿Se puede parar de pie por solo unos minutos?
seh PWEH-deh pah-RAR deh PEE-eh pohr SOH-loh OOnos mee-NOOtos

Can you…

¿Puede usted…
PWEH-deh oosTED

…stand up?

…pararse?
pahRAHR-seh

…sit down?

…siéntese?
…seeEN-teh-seh

…lie down?

…acuéstese?
…ah-KOOESteh-seh

…lift/raise your hand?

…levantar la mano?
…leh-banTAR las MAH-nos

…move your head?

…mover la cabeza?
…moh-BER lah kah-BEHsah

Stand here.

Párese aqui.
PAHreh-seh ah-KEE

Stand straight.

Párese derecho.
PAHreh-seh deh-REHchoh

Stand up.

Póngase de pie.
PONgah-seh deh PEE-eh

Hold here.

Aguanta aquí.
ah-GWANtah ah-KEE

Put your chin here.

Coloque la barbilla aquí.
koh-LOHkeh lah bar-BEEyah ah-KEE

Bend (or lean) forward.

Recuéstese hacia el frente.
-or- hacia adelante
reh-KWESteh-seh AH-seeah el FREN-teh/ AH-seeah ah-deh-LANteh

Bend (or lean) backward.	*Recuéstese hacia atrás.* reh-KWESteh-seh AH-seeah ah-TRAS
Step back.	*Échese para atrás.* EHcheh-seh PAH-rah ah-TRAS
Step forward.	*Échese para delante.* EHcheh-seh PAH-rah deh-LANteh
Step away…	*Mantenga…* man-TENgah…
…from the machine	*…lejos de la máquina* …leh-hos deh lah MAHkee-nah
Sit…please.	*Siéntese…por favor.* seeEN-teh-seh..pohr fah-BOHR
…here…	*…aquí…* ah-KEE
…on the table…	*…en la mesa…* en lah MEH-sah
…on this chair…	*…en la silla…* en lah SEE-jah
…over here…	*…aquí…* ah-KEE
…over there…	*…allá…* …ah-JAH
Do not move	*No se mueva* noh seh mooEH-bah
Do not move once I have positioned you.	*No se mueva una vez que yo lo ponga en posición.* noh seh MOOEH-bah oona bes keh joh loh PON-gah en poh-see-SEEON
Please put your hand here.	*Coloque -or- ponga la mano aquí, por favor.* koh-LOHkeh/PON-gah lah MAH-noh ah-KEE, pohr fab-BOHR
Put your hands …	*Coloque las manos…* koh-LOHkeh las MAH-nos…

...above your head.	*...encima de la cabeza.* ...en-SEEmah deh lah kah-BEHsah
...by your side.	*...por el lado.* ...pohr el LAH-doh
Take your hands away from...	*Mantenga las manos lejos del...* man-TENgah las MAH-nos LEHhos del...
...your chest.	*...pecho.* ...PEH-choh
...your stomach.	*...estómago.* ...es-TOHmah-goh
Keep your hands together.	*Mantenga las manos juntas/os** man-TENgah las MAH-nos HOON-tas/os
Take your hand off.	*Saque la mano.* SAH-keh lah MAH-noh
Lift both hands.	*Levante ambas manos.* leh-BANteh AM-bas MAH-nos
Do not hold here.	*No aguante aquí.* noh ah-GWANteh ah-KEE
Please hold... here.	*Por favor aguantate...aquí.* pohr fah-BOHR ah-gwan-TAHteh...ah-KEE
...this bar	*...esta barra* ..ES-tah BAHR-rah
Hold here...	*Aguanta aquí...* ah-GWANtah ah-KEE
...with both hands.	*...con ambas manos.* ...con AM-bas MAH-nos
...with your right hand.	...con la mano derecha. ...con lah MAH-noh deh-REHchah
...with your left hand.	*...con la mano izquierda.* ...con lah MAH-noh ees-KEYEER-dah

Bend your elbow.	*Dobla el codo.* DOH-blah ...el KOH-doh
Sit up. (to someone slouching)	*Incorpórese -or- siéntese hacia delante* een-kor-POHreh-seh / seeEN-teh-seh AH-seeah deh-LANteh
Sit back.(or move back).	*Siéntese para hacia atrás.* seeEN-teh-seh PAH-rah AH-seeah ah-TRAS
Move your shoulder forwards	*Mueva el hombro hacia el frente* mooEH-bah el OM-broh ah-SEEah el FREN-teh
Please move back a step	*Por favor muévase para atrás* pohr fah-BOHR mooeh-BAHseh PAH-rah AH-tras
Bend at your waist only	*Doble a la cintura solamente* DOH-bleh ah lah seen-TOOrah soh-lah-MENteh
Do not ...lean forwards	*No...eche hacia el frente* noh ...EH-cheh ah-SEEah el FREN-teh
...bend your knees	*..doble las rodillas* ...DOH-bleh las roh-DEEjas
Keep... your head up	*Mantenga...la cabeza arriba* man-TENgah ...lah kah-BEHsah ah-REEbah
...your hand down	*...la mano abajo* *...lah MAH-noh ah-*BAHhoh
Turn your head ...	Mueva la cabeza... mooEH-bah lah kah-BEHsah...
...to the left/right	*...a la derecha/izquierda* ...ah lah deh-REHchah/ ees-KEYEERdah
...away from the machine	*...lejos de la máquina* ...LEH-hos deh lah MAHkee-nah

OTHER NECESSARY INSTRUCTIONS

Here is...	*Aquí está...* ah-KEE es-TAH
...a pillow.	*...la almohada.* lah al-moh-AHdah
Not like that.	*No es como eso.* noh es KOH-moh ES-oh
Yes, like that.	*Sí, es como eso.* see es KOH-moh ES-oh
No, like this.	*No, como esto.* noh KOH-moh ES-toh
That's fine.	*Eso está bien.* ES-oh es-TAH BEEen
O.K.	*Está bien.* es-TAH BEEen
That's not right.	*No está bien.* noh es-TAH BEEen
Step down.	*Bájese.* BAHeh-seh
Step up.	*Súbase.* SOObah-seh
Please wait for me here.	*Espérame aquí, por favor.* es-PEHrah-meh ah-KEE, pohr fah-BOHR
Stay here.	*Quédese aquí.* KEHdeh-seh ah-KEE
Wait here for a few minutes.	*Espera aquí unos minutos.* es-PEHrah ah-KEE OOnos mee-NOOtos
Do not leave the room.	*No deje el cuarto -or-* *No salga del cuarto.* noh DEHeh el KWAR-toh (noh SAL-gah del KWAR-toh)

I will be back in a few minutes.	*Regreso en poco minutos.* reh-GREHsoh en POH-koh mee-NOOtos
Do not touch...	*No toque...* noh TOH-keh...
...here/there.	*...aquí/ allá.* ...ah-KEE/ah-JAH
...anything.	*...alguna cosa.* ...ahl-GOOnah KOH-sah
Keep the gown on.	*Déjese la bata puesta.* DEHeh-seh lah BAH-tah PWES tah
Put your clothes on.	*Póngase la ropa.* PONgah-seh lah ROH-pah
Let me help you	*Dejeme ayudarle* DEH-heh-meh ah-joo-DARleh
The study is over now	*El estudio terminó.* el es-TOOdee-oh ter-meeNOH
You can...leave now	*Usted puede...irse ahora* oosTED PWEH-doh...EER-seh ah-OHrah
...go	*...irse* ...EER-seh
...put your clothes on	*...Pongase la ropa* ...POHNgah-seh lah ROH-pah
Someone will take you...	*Alguien lo lleva ...* AHL-giehn loh JEH-bah...
...upstairs.	*...arriba.* ah-REEbah
...to your room.	*...a su cuarto.* ah soo KWAR-toh
You will be taken to your room shortly.	*Pronto lo suben a su cuarto.* PRON-toh loh SOO-ben ah soo KWAR-toh

POSSIBLE RESPONSES

I can't.	*No puedo.* noh PWEH-doh
I have...	*Tengo...* TEN-goh...
...pain in my left/right shoulder.	*...dolor en el hombro izquierdo/derecho.* doh-LOR en el OM-broh ees-KEYEERdoh/ deh-REHchoh
I cannot ...	*No puedo...* noh PWEH-doh
...move.	*moverme.* moh-BERmeh
...stand.	*...pararme.* pah-RARmeh
...sit down.	*...sentarme.* sen-TARmeh
...walk.	*...caminar.* kah-mehNAR

**Use "o" for the masculine and "a" for the feminine.*

PATIENT EVALUATION

GENERAL

See Chapter on filling out forms.

What is your ...	*¿Cuál es su...* kwal es soo
...age.	*...edad.* eh-DAD
...temperature?	*...temperatura?* tem-pehrah-TOO-rah
...weight?	*...peso?* PEH-soh
...height?	*...altura?* al-TOOrah
Please can you...	*¿Por favor podría usted...* pohr fah-BOHR poh-DREEah oosTED
...write it down?	*...escríbalo?* es-kree-BAHloh
...speak more slowly	*...hablar más lento?* ab-LAR mas LEN-toh
On what date (day) did you have the accident?	*¿Cuándo qué el día accidente?* KWAN-doh KEH el DEE-ah ahk-seeDEN-teh
Do you have a sore throat?	*¿Tiene dolor de garganta?* tee-ENeh doh-LOHR deh gar-GANtah
Do you have ...	*¿Tiene usted...* tee-ENeh oos-TED
...arthritis?	*...artritis?* ahr-TREEtees

...incontinence?	*...incontinencia?* eekon-tee-nenSEE-ah
...bood in your urine?	*...sangre en la orina?* SAHN-greh en lah oh-REEnah
...chest pain?	...dolor de pecho? doh-LOHR deh PEH-choh
...constipation?	*...constipación/estreñimiento?* kohns-tee-pahSEE-ON/ es-treh-nyee-MEE-ENtoh
... a cough?	...un catarro? oon kah-TAHRrah
...difficulty swallowing?	*...dificultad tragando?* dee-fee-koolTAHD trah-GANdoh
...difficulty urinating?	*...dificultad urinado?* dee-fee-koolTAHD on-reeNAH-doh
... agoiter?	*...un bocio?* oon boh-SEEoh
...any heart problem?	*...algún problems del corazón?* ahl-GOON proh-BLEMah del kon-rahSOH
...high blood pressure?	*...presión sanguinea alta?* preh-SEEON san-GIHneh-ah AL-tah
... any pain?	*...dolor?* doh-LOHR
...sinusitis	*...sinositis?* see-nohSEE-tees
...any swelling?	*algún hinchazón?* ahl-GOON een-chahSOHN
How long have you had...	*¿Cuándo tiempo ha tenido...* QWAN-toh teeEM-poh ah teh-NEEdoh
...the pain	...el dolor? el doh-LOHR

Are you…	¿Es usted … es oosTED
…anemic?	*…anémico/a?** ah-NEHmee-koh
… diabetic?	*…diabético/a?** dee-ah-BEHtee-koh
Do you have any…	*¿Tiene algún…* tee-ENeh ahl-GOON
…anxiety attacks?	*…problema de ansiedad?* proh-BLEMah deh ahn-see-ehDAD
…memory problems?	*…pérdida de memoria?* PEHRdee-dah deh meh-MOHree-ah
…mood swings?	*…problema de combios de temperamento?* proh-BLEMah deh kohm-BEEos deh tehm-peh-rah-MENtoh
…sleep problems?	*…problema al dormir?* proh-BLEMah al dorMEER
Have you had any siezures?	*¿Ha tenido usted algún desmayo?* ah tee-NEEdoh oosTED ahl-GOON dehs-MAHjoh
Do you have a history of ashma?	*¿Tiene historial de asma?* teeEN-eh ees-torREEal deh HAHS-mah
Do you know what test/study you are having?	*¿Sabe usted el estudio que tiene?* SAH-beh oosTED el es-TOOdee-oh keh TEE-ENeh
Why are you having this study?	*¿Porque esta tomando este estudio?* POHR-keh es-TAH toh-MANdoh ES-teh es-TOOdee-oh
Was this study explained to you?	*¿Le explicaron el estudio?* leh ex-plee-KAHron el es-TOOdee-oh

What type of surgery did you have?	*¿Que operacion se ha hecho?* keh oh-peh-rah-SEEON seh ah EH-choh
Have you ever had any surgery or operations…	*¿Se ha operado algúna vez…* seh ah oh-peh-RAHdoh ahl GOONah bes
…on your stomach?	*…en el estómago?* en el es-TOHmah-goh
…on your colon/intestines?	*en el colon/intestino?* en el KOH-lon / een-tes-TEEnoh
Have you been vomiting?	*¿Ha estado usted vomitando?* ah esTAH-doh oosTED boh-meeTANdoh
Have you had a… before?	*¿Ha tenido que tomar antes…?* ah teh-NEEdoh keh toh-MAR AN-tehs…
Have you been vomitting..	*¿Ha tenido vomito…* ah teh-NEEdoh BOHmee-toh
…after meals?	*…despues de las comidas?* …dehs-POOES deh las coh-MEEdas
Did you eat anything this morning?	*¿Comió usted algo esta mañana?* koh-MEEOH oosTED AHL-goh ES-tah mah-NYAHnah
Did you eat breakfast?	*¿Se desayunó?* seh deh-sah-jooNOH
Did you take an enema…?	*¿Se puso una enema…?* seh POO-soh oona ehNEH-mah
…last night	*…anoche* …ah-NOHcheh
…this morning	*…esta manana* …ES-tah mah-NYAHnah
…yesterday	*…ayer* …ah-JEHR

Do you have any pain...?

¿Tiene dolor ...?
teeEN-eh doh-LOR

... in your back

...en la espalda
...en lah es-PALdah

...in your bladder

...en la vejiga
...en lah beh-HEEgah

Did you follow the prep instructions that you were given?

¿Siguio usted las instrucciones para la preparacion que se le entrego?
seeGIH-OH oosTED las eens-trook-SEEONes PAH-rah lah preh-pah-rah-SEEON keh seh leh en-trehGOH

You are having an IVP...

Va a tener el estudio IVP...
bah ah tenEHR el es-TOOdeeoh IVP (ee beh peh)

..today

...hoy
...oi

...this morning

...en esta manana
...en ES-tah mah-NYAHnah

Have you had a barium meal before?

¿Ha tenido que tomar antes bario?
ah teh-NEEdoh keh toh-MAR AN-tehs BAHree-oh

I will give you a painkiller.
koh

Le daré un analgéscio
leh dah-REH oon ahnal-GEHsee-

The doctor will give the injection

El doctor lo va a inyectar
el doc-TOHR loh bah ah een-jekTAHR

The doctor will put a plaster on.

El doctor le va a poner un yeso.
el docTOHR leh vah ah poh-NER oon YEEH-soh.

The doctor will see you.

El doctor lo verá.
el doc-TOHR loh beh-RAH

The doctor will look at your leg...	*El doctor le verá la pierna...* el doc-TOHR leh beh-RAH lah PEE-ERnah
...now.	*...ahora.* ah-OHrah
...in a few minutes.	*...en unos minutos.* en OOnos meeNOOtos
The doctor will be conducting this test.	*El doctor va a estar a cargo del estudio.* el doc-TOHR bah ah es-TAR ah KAR-goh del es-TOOdee-oh
The doctor will be here...	*El doctor estará aquí...* el doc-tohr es-tarRAH ah-KEE
...in a little while.	*...en un momento* en oon moh-MENtoh
...in ten minutes.	*...en diez minutos.* en dee-es mee-NOOtos
...soon.	*...pronto.* PRON-toh
Your leg is broken.	*Su pierna está rota.* soo PEE-ERnah esTAH ROH-tah
You sprained your wrist.	*Se dobló la muñeca.* seh dohb-LOH lah moo-NYEHkah
It's dislocated.	*Está dislocado.* es-TAH dees-lohKAH-doh
I want you to have a x-ray taken.	*Quiero que le hagan una radiografía/placa* kee-EERoh keh leh AH-gan OOnah rah-deeoh-grah-FEEah/PLAH-kahs
This wound must be stiched up.	*La herida tiene que cosérse.* lah ehr-REEdah tee-ENeh keh kohSEHRseh
You will have to be admitted (to the hospital)	*Lo van a internar.* loh ban ah een-tehrNAR

You may need surgery.	*Puede nesecitar cirugía/operación.* PWEHdeh neh-seh-seeTAR see-rooGEE-ah/oh-peh-rahSEE-ON
We must keep you here for a few hours.	*Lo tenemos que mantener aquí por algunas horas.* loh teh-NEHmos keh mahn-tehNER ah-KEE pohr alGOON-as OH-ahs
You will not be able to drive home after this exam	*(Usted) no podria manejar depues del estudio* (oosted) noh poh-DREEah mah-nehJAR dehs-POOES del es-TOOdee-oh
Does your husband/wife know that you are here?	*¿Su esposo/a sabe que está aquí?** soo es-POHsoh/sah SAH-beh keh esTAH ah-KEE
Would you like to call your home?	*¿Quiere llamar a su casa?* kee-EERreh jah-MAR ah soo KAH-sah
This is a concent form.	*Éste es un consentimiento.* ES-teh es oon kon-sen-teeMEE-ENtoh
Please read this.	*Por favor, lea esto.* pohr fah-BOHR, LEHah ES-toh
Please sign here.	*Por favor, firme aquí.* pohr fah-BOHR, FEER-meh ah-KEE
Please sign this consent form.	*Por favor, firme este consentimiento.* pohr fah-BOHR, FEER-meh ESteh kon-sen-teeMEE-ENtoh
I need your consent for this study.	*Necesito su consentimiento para este estudio.* neh-seh-SEEtoh suh con-sen-teeMEE-ENtoh PAH-rah ES-teh es-TOOdee-oh

I will get someone to explain this study to you.

(Yo) podría conseguir a alguien que le explique este estudio.
(joh) poh-DREEah kon-seh-GEER ah AHL-giehn keh leh ek-PLEEkeh ES-teh esTOO-deeoh

This is the concent form for this study.

Éste es el consentimiento para este estudio.
ES-teh es el kon-sen-teeMEE-ENtoh PAH-rah ES-teh es-TOOdee-oh

You will not be able to drive home after this exam.

(Usted) no podría manejar depués del estudio.
(oosTED) noh poh-DREEah mah-nehJAR dehs-POOES del es-TOOdee-oh

POSSIBLE RESPONSES

My temperature is 100 degrees.

Tengo cien grados de temperatura.
TEHN-goh see-en GRAH-dos deh tem-pehr-rahTOOrah

I've been vomiting.

He tenido vómitos.
eh tehNEEdoh BOHmee-tos

I am...

Estoy...
es-TOY

I've got...

Tengo...
TEHN-goh

My blood pressure is too high/low.

Mi presión sanguínea es demasiado alta/baja.
mee preh-SEE-ON san-GIHneh-ah es deh-mahSEE-AHdoh AH-tah/BAH-hah

FEMALE EVALUATION

Are you pregnant?	*¿Está usted embarazada?* es-TAH oosTED em-bah-rah-SAHdah
At what age did your period begin?	*¿A qué edad tuvo su primer periodo menstrual?* ah KEH eh-DAD too-voh soo pree-mehr pehr-REE OH-doh men-stroo-AL
When was your last peroid? menstrual?	*¿Cuándo qué su último periodo* QWAN-doh KEH soo OOLtee-moh pehr-REE-OHdoh
Is your period regular?	*¿Es su periodo menstrual regular?* es soo pehr-REE-OHdoh mens-stroo-AL reh-gooLAR
Any spotting between periods?	*¿Algún sangrado entre periodos?* ahl-GOON sahn-GRAHdoh ENtreh pehr-REE-OHdos
What age did menopause begin?	*¿A qué edad comenzó su menopausia?* ah KEH eDAD koh-mehnZOH soo meh-noh-PAUseeah
When was your last	*¿Cuándo qué su último ...* QWANdoh KEH soo OLtee-moh
...pelvic examination?	*...exámen pélvico?* ekAH-men PEHLbee-koh
...pap test?	*...prueba de cáncer en la cérvix?* prooWEH-bah deh KAHN-ser en lah SER-beek
Have you had any pregnancies?	*¿Ha estado usted embarazada alguna vez?* ah esTAHdoh oosTED em-bah-rah-SAHdah alGOON-ah bes
...any still births?	*...alguna nacido muerto?* alGOON-ah nah-SEEdoh MWER-toh

How many live births?

¿Cuántos embarazos logrados?
QWAN-tos em-bah-RAHsos loh-GRAHdos

Have you had any abortions?

¿Ha tenido algún aborto?
ah tehNEEdoh ahl-GOON ahBORtoh

POSSIBLE RESPONSES

I have a vaginal infection

Tengo una infección vaginal.
TEHN-goh OOnah een-fek-SEE-ON bah-geeNAL

I am on the pill.

Tomo la píldora.
TOHmoh lah PEELdoh-rah

**Use "o" for the masculine and "a" for the feminine.*

PREPARATION STUDIES

GIVING AN INTRAVENOUS

The doctor will give the injection	*El doctor lo va a inyectar* el doc-TOHR loh bah ah een-jekTAHR
Please let us know if you feel sick....	*Por favor, dejenos saber si se siente enfermo....* pohr fah-BOHR, deh-HEHnos sah-BEHR see seh seeEN-teh en-FEHRmoh
...after the injection	*...despues de la inyeccion* ...dehs-POOES deh lah een-jek-SEEON
You may feel sick after you are injected	*Puede que se sienta enfermo despues de ser inyectado* PWEH-doh keh seh seeEN-tah en-FEHRmoh dehs-POOES deh sehr een-jek-TAHdoh
Relax the test will be over...	*Tranquiliseze el estudio se terminara....* trahn-kee-LEEsee-seh el es-TOOdee-oh se ter-mee-nahRAH
....soon	*...pronto* ...PRON-toh
...in half an hour	*...en media hora* ...en meh-DEEah OH-rah
You will have to lie on this table...	*Usted tendra que acostarse en esta mesa....* oosted TEHN-drah keh ah-kohs-TAHRseh en ES-tah MEH-sah
...for half an hour	*...media hora* ...meh-DEEah OH-rah
...during the study	*...durante el estudio* ...doo-RANteh el es-TOOdee-oh

Do not... sit up	*No se... siente* noh seh....seeEN-teh
...lie down	*...acueste* ...ah-KOOESteh
...turn on your side	*...mueva de lado* ...MOO-EHbah deh LAH-doh
Let me help you	*Dejeme ayudarle* DEH-heh-meh ah-joo-DARleh
Please go to the bathroom and urinate	*Por favor vaya al bano y orine* pohr fab-BOHR BAH-jah al BAH-nyoh ee oh-REEneh
Go to the bathroom, urinate then come back	*Vaya al bano, orine y luego regrese* BAH-jah al BAN-nyoh, oh-REEneh ee looEH-goh reh-GREHseh
Please urinate then lie on your back on the table	*Por favor orine, luego acuestese boca arriba en la mesa* pohr fah-BOHR oh-REEneh, looEH-goh ah-KOOESteh-seh BOH-kah ah-REEbah en lah MEH-sah
Please urinate now	*Por favor orine ahora* pohr fah-BOHR oh-REEneh ah-OHrah
Please try again	*Por favor trate otra vez* pohr fah-BOHR TRAH-teh OT-rah behs
Wait a few minutes and try again	*Espere unos minutos y trate otra vez* es-PEHreh OOnos mee-NOOtos ee TRAH-teh OT-rah behs
The toilet is this way	*El bano esta aqui* el BAH-nyoh es-TAH ah-KEE

POSSIBLE RESPONSES

I can't	*No puedo* noh PWEH-doh
I tried but couldn't	*Yo trate pero no puedo* joh trah-TEH PEH-roh noh PWEH-doh
I can't urinate	*no puedo orinar* noh PWEH-doh oh-reeNAR

CONTRAST STUDIES

Hold this (point)	*Sostenga esto -or- aguante esto@* (sohs-TENgah ES-toh) ah-GWANteh ES-toh
Do not drink …	*No tome…* noh TOH-meh…
Do not swallow…	*No trague…* noh TRAH-geh…
….until we tell you to	*…hasta le diremos* …AHS-tah leh dee-REHmos
…until the doctor tells you to	*…hasta el doctor le dira* …AHS-tah el doc-TOHR leh dee-RAH
Drink the liquid…now	*Tomese el líquido…ahora.* TOHmeh-seh el LEEkee-doh…ah-OHrah
Drink now	*Tome ahora* TOH-meh ah-OHrah
Drink some more	*Tome un poco mas* TOH-meh oon POH-coh mas

Swallow some more	*Trague mas* TRAH-geh mas
Start drinking now	*Empieze a tomar ahora* em-PEE-EHseh ah toh-MAR ah-OHrah
Stop drinking	*Pare de tomar* PAH-reh deh toh-MAR
Drink... faster/slower	*Tome... mas rapido/mas lento* TOH-meh... mas RAHpee-doh/ mas LEN-toh
Take a little and hold it in your mouth	*Aguanta un poco en la boca* ah-GWANtah oon POH-koh en lah BOH-kah
Take a big mouthful and hold it in your mouth	*Coje mucho y aguantalo en la boca* KOH-heh MOO-choh ee ah-GWANtah-loh en lah BOH-kah
Cough, please	*Tosa, por favor* TOH-sah, pohr fah-BOHR
Put your hands ...	*Coloque las manos...* koh-LOHkeh las MAH-nos...
...above your head	*...encima de la cabeza* ...en-SEEmah deh lah kah-BEHsah
...by your side	*...por el lado* ...pohr el LAH-doh
Take your hands away from...	*Mantenga las manos lejos del...* man-TENgah las MAH-nos LEH-hos del...
...your chest	*...pecho* ...PEH-choh
...your stomach	*...estomago* ..es-TOHmah-goh
Turn on...	*Coloquese..* koh-LOHkeh-seh...

…your side(right/left)

…el lado (derecho/izquierdo)
…el LAH-doh
(deh-REHchoh/ees-KEYEERdoh

…your back (face up)

…boca arriba
…BOH-kah ah-REEbah

…your stomach (face down)

…boca abajo
…BOH-kah ah-BAHoh

POSSIBLE COMMENTS

I cannot swallow	*No puedo tragar* noh PWEH-doh trah-GAHR
I can't drink any more	*No puedo beber mas* noh PWEH-doh beh-BEHR mas
I can't drink while lying down	*No puedo beber mientras estoy recostada* noh PWEH-doh beh-BEHR meeEN-trahs es-TOY reh-kohs-TAHdah

ENEMAS

I am going to insert a tube in your rectum	*Voy a colocar el tubo en el recto* boy ah koh-lohCAR el TOOB-oh en el REK-toh
I am going to insert the tube now	*Voy a insertar o colocar el tubo ahora* boy ah een-serTAHR oh koh-lohCAR el TOOB-oh ah-OHrah
The liquid is going in now	*El líquido esta entrando* el LEEkee-doh es-TAH en-TRANdoh
Do not try to push the tube out	*No trate de pujar el tubo* noh TRAH-teh deh poo-HAR el TOOB-oh
Do not try to evacuate	No trate de evacuar noh TRAH-teh deh eh-bah-kooAR
Do not evacuate	No evacue noh eh-bah-KOOeh
Please try to hold the barium/liquid in	Por favor trate de retener el bario/líquido pohr fah-BOHR TRAH-teh deh reh-tehNEHR el BAHree-oh/ LEEkee-doh

Please hold it in

Aguante esto
ah-GWANteh ES-toh

It will be uncomfortable

Va hacer un poco incómodo
bah ah-SEHR oon POH-koh een-KOHmoh-doh

The exam will last about…

El estudio toma alrededor de…
el es-TOOdee-oh TOH-mah al-reh-dehDOR deh…

… ten minutes

… diez minutos
…dee-es mee-NOOtos

We will not put all of the Barium/liquid in your colon

No vamos a colocarle todo el bario/líquido en el colon
noh BAH-mos ah koh-loh-CARleh TOH-doh el BAHree-oh/LEEkee-doh en el KOH-lon

We will be filling up your colon with the barium

Nosotros llenaremos el colon de bario
noh-SOHtros jeh-nah-REHmos el KOH-lon deh BAHree-oh

The barium is going in now

El bario esta entrando
el BAHree-oh es-TAH en-TRANdoh

The doctor will be monitoring this study

El doctor estara a cargo de este estudio
el doc-TOHR es-tahRAH ah KAHR-goh deh ES-teh es-TOOdee-oh

Do not move

No se mueva
noh seh mooEH-bah

Only some of the barium will fill your colon

Solo un poco de bario va a llenar el colon
SOH-loh oon POH-koh deh BAHree-oh bah ah jeh-NAR el KOH-lon

I will allow you to go to the bathroom in a few minutes

Yo lo dejare ir al bano en unos pocos minutos
joh loh deh-harREH eer al BAH-nyoh en OOnos POH-kos mee-NOOtos

Please try to …	*Por favor, trate…* pohr fah-BOHR, TRAH-teh…
…relax	*…de relajarse* …deh reh-lah-HARseh
…to hold it in	*…de aguantar o retener el bario* …deh ah-GWANtar oh reh-tehnNEHR el BAHree-oh
Breathe through your mouth.	*Coja aire por la boca* KOH-hah AY-reh pohr lah BOH-kah
I am removing the tube now	*Estoy removiendo el tubo ahora* es-TOY reh-mohBEE-ENdoh el TOOB-oh ah-OHrah
I will remove the tube in a few minutes	*Le quitare el tubo* *en unos minutos* leh kee-tarREH el TOOB-oh en oonos mee-NOOtos
You can go to the bathroom..	*Usted puede ir al bano…* oosTED PWEH-deh eer al BAH-nyoh
…now	*…ahora* …ah-OHrah
…in a few minutes	*…en pocos minutos* …en POH-kos mee-NOOtos
…after I remove the tube	*…despues que remueva el tubo* …dehs-POOES keh reh-mooEH-bah el TOOB-oh
You can evacuate the barium in the bathroom	*Usted puede evacuar el bario en* *el bano* oosTED PWEH-deh eh-bah-kooAR el BAHree-oh en el BAH-nyoh
The barium is flowing back into the bag	*El bario esta bajando a* *la bolsa otra vez* el BAHree-oh es-TAH bah-HANdoh ah lah BOHL-sah OT-rah bes

You can relax now, the test is almost over	*Se puede tranquilezar ahora, el estudio esta casi terminado* seh PWEH-deh tran-kee-leh-SAR ah-OHrah, el es-TOOdee-oh es-TAH kah-SEE ter-mee-NAHdoh
The barium may make you constipated	*El bario te puede poner estrenido /constipado@* el BAHree-oh teh PWEH-deh ponEHR es-treh-NEEdoh / kon-stee-PAHdoh
You must drink plenty of fluids or water …	*Debe tomar bastante liquido o agua ….* DEH-beh toh-MAR bas-TANteh LEEkee-doh o AH-gwah
…tomorrow	*…manana* …mah-NYAH-nah
…tonight	*…esta noche* …ES-tah NOH-cheh

POSSIBLE RESPONSES

I cannot hold it any longer	*No puedo aguantar mas* noh PWEH-doh ah-GWANtar mas
I need to go to the bathroom	Necesito ir al bano neh-seh-SEEtoh eer al BAH-nyoh
It is coming out	Esta saliendo es-TAH sah-leeENdoh
Please stop	Por favor pare pohr fah-BOHR PAH-reh
I don't feel well	No me siento bien noh meh seeEN-toh beeEN
I will never be able to hold so much barium inside of me	Yo nunca podre aguanta tanto bario dentro joh NOON-kah POH-dreh ah-GWANtah TAN-toh BAHree-oh DEN-troh

@ either word is acceptable

TAKING MAMMOGRAMS
GENERAL QUESTIONS AND EXPRESSIONS

Are you pregnant?

¿Esta usted embarazada?
es-TAH oosTED em-bah-rah-SAHdah

Have you had x-rays of your breast before?

¿Ha tenido algun mamograma anteriormente?
ah teh-NEEdoh ahl-GOON mah-moh-GRAHmah an-teh-reeor-MENteh

...When?

...¿Cuando?
...QWAN-doh

...Where?

...¿Donde?
...DON-deh

Where were the x-rays taken?

¿En donde le tomaron los radiografias?
en DON-deh leh toh-mahRON los rah-deeoh-grah-FEEas

At...?

¿En...?
en...

Hospital or Clinic or Doctor's office

Hospital o clinica u oficina de doctor
ohs-peeTAL oh clee-NEEkah oo oh-fee-SEEnah deh doc-TOHR

Please can you...?

¿Por favor podria usted...?
pohr fah-BOHR poh-DREEah oosTED

...write it down

...escribalo
...es-cree-BAHloh

...speak more slowly

...hablar mas lento
...ab-LAR mas LEN-toh

Is this a routine exam?

¿Es un estudio de rutina?
es oon es-TOOdee-oh deh roo-TEEnah

Is there something wrong...?	*¿Hay algo malo...?* ahee AHL-goh MAH-loh
...with your breast	*...con el seno* ...kon el SEN-noh
Why you are having this exam?	*¿Cuales la causa del estudio?* qwah-les lah KAH-OOsah del es-TOOdee-oh
Do you have pain in your breast?	*¿Tiene usted dolor en el seno?* teeEN-eh oosTED doh-LOR en el SEH-noh
...a lump?	*...una masa?* ...oona MAH-sah
...any nipple discharge?	...alguna secrecion por el pezon? ...ahl-GOONah seh-kreh-SEEON pohr el peh-SOHN
How long have you had...?	*¿Cuanto tienpo ha tenido...?* QWAN-toh teeEM-poh ah teh-NEEdoh
...the pain	*...el dolor* ...el doh-LOR
...the lump	*...la masa* ...lah MAH-sah
...the discharge	*...la secrecion* ...lah seh-kreh-SEEON
This is a routine exam	*Este es un estudio de rutina* ES-teh es oon es-TOOdee-oh deh roo-TEEnah
I will be taking two x-rays of each breast	*Voy a tomarle dos radiografias/ placas# de cada seno* boy ah toh-MARleh dos rah-deeoh-grah-FEEas/ PLAH-kas deh KAH-dah SEH-noh
I will have to compress your breast for this study	*Tengo que apretar el seno en este estudio* TEN-goh keh ah-prehTAR el SEH-noh en ES-teh es-TOOdee-oh

I am going to compress your breast	*Voy a apretarle el seno* boy ah ah-preh-TARleh el SEH-noh
Have a seat	*Tome asiento -or- Sientese* TOH-meh ah-seeEN-toh -- seeEN-teh-seh
Stand here	*Parese aqui* PAHreh-seh ah-KEE
Please hold... here	*Por favor aguantate...aqui* pohr fah-BOHR ah-gwan-TAHteh...ah-KEE
...this bar	*...esta barra* ...ES-tah BAHR-rah
Move your shoulder forwards	*Mueva el hombro hacia el frente* mooEH-bah el OM-broh ah-SEEah el FREN-teh
Do not hold here	*No aguante aqui* noh ah-GWANteh ah-KEE
Please move back a step	*Por favor muevase para atras* pohr fah-BOHR mooeh-BAHseh PAH-rah AH-tras
Step back	*Echese para atras* EHcheh-seh PAH-rah AH-tras
Step forwards	*Echese para delante* EHcheh-seh PAH-rah deh-LANteh
Step away...	*Mantenga...* man-TENgah...
...from the machine	*...lejos de la maquina* ...leh-hos deh lah MAHkee-nah
Take out your breast (from the machine)	*Saque el seno* SAH-keh el SEH-noh
Do not move	*No se mueva* noh seh mooEH-bah
Lift your right/left arm	*Levanta el brazo derecho/izquierdo* leh-BANtah el BRAH-soh deh-REHchoh/ees-KEYEERdoh

Bend at your waist only	*Doble a la cintura solamente* DOH-bleh ah lah seen-TOOrah soh-lah-MENteh
Do not …lean forwards	*No…eche hacia el frente* noh …EH-cheh ah-SEEah el FREN-teh
…bend your knees	*…doble las rodillas* …DOH-bleh las roh-DEEjas
Keep… your head up	*Mantenga…la cabeza arriba* man-TENgah …lah kah-BEHsah ah-REEbah
…your hand down	*…la mano abajo* …lah MAH-noh ah-BAHhoh
Turn your head …	*Mueva la cabeza…* mooEH-bah lah kah-BEHsah…
…to the left/right	*…a la derecha/izquierda* …ah lah deh-REHchah/ ees-KEYEERdah
…away from the machine	*…lejos de la maquina* …LEH-hos deh lah MAHkee-nah
Come this way	*Venga aca* BEN-gah ah-KAH
The study is over now	*El estudio termino* el es-TOOdee-oh ter-meeNOH
You can…leave now	*Usted puede…irse ahora* oosTED PWEH-doh…EER-seh ah-OHrah
…go	*…irse* …EER-seh
…put your clothes on	…Pongase la ropa …POHNgah-seh lah ROH-pah

POSSIBLE RESPONSE

No, I took it at...	*No, ya tomaron unas en...* noh, jah toh-MAHron oonas en...
I have...	*Tengo...* TEN-goh...
...a lump	*...una masa* ...oona MAH-sah
...pain in both breast	*...dolor en ambos senos* ...doh-LOR en AM-bos SEH-nos
...a nipple discharge	*...secrecion por el pezon* ...seh-kreh-SEEON pohr el peh-SON
..pain in my left/right breast	*Dolor en el seno izquierdo/ derecho* doh-LOR en el SEH-noh ees-KEYEERdoh/ deh-REHchoh
I have had it for...	*Yo he tenido esto por...* joh eh teh-NEEdoh ES-toh pohr...

 # Although it is the incorrect Spanish word, "placa" is commonly used to refer to an x-ray.

BEDSIDE NURSING
DAILY CARE

You must drink plenty of fluids or water ...	*Debe tomar bastante liquido o agua ....* DEH-beh toh-MAR bas-TANteh LEEkee-doh o AH-gwah
...tomorrow	*...mañana* ...mah-NYAH-nah
...tonight	*...esta noche* ...ES-tah NOH-cheh
You cannot have any...	*Usted no puede tomar...* oos-TED noh pweh-deh to-MAR
...liquids.	*...líquidos.* LEEkee-doh
...water.	*...agua.* AH-gwah
...food.	*comida.* koh-MEEdah
You cannot eat anything.	*No puede comer nada.* noh PWEH-deh koh-MER NAHdah
You can have only ice chips.	*Puede comer sólo hielo.* PWEH-deh koh-MER SOHloh YEEHloh
Relax, the test will be over...	*Tranquiliseze, el estudio se terminará....* trahn-kee-LEEsee-seh el es-TOOdee-oh se ter-mee-nahRAH
....soon	*...pronto* ...PRON-toh
...in half an hour	*...en media hora* ...en meh-DEEah OH-rah

You will have to lie on this table…	*Usted tendra que acostarse en esta mesa….* oosTED TEHN-drah keh ah-kohs-TAHRseh en ES-tah MEH-sah
…for half an hour	*…media hora* …meh-DEEah OH-rah
…during the study	*…durante el estudio* …doo-RANteh el es-TOOdee-oh
Let me help you	*Dejeme ayudarle* DEH-heh-meh ah-joo-DARleh
Do not remove…	*No remueva…* noh reh-MOOEH-bah
…the bandage.	*…el vendaje.* …el ben-DAHheh
Where does it hurt?	*¿Dónde le duele?* DON-deh le DWEL-eh
Does it hurt here? (point)	*¿Le duele aquí?* le DWEL-eh ah-KEE
Did you hurt your hand?	*¿Le duele la mano?* le DWEL-eh lah MAH-noh
I want to examine you.	*Quiero examinarlo.* kee-EERoh ek-ahmee-NARloh
Please sit up on the bed.	*Por favor siéntese en la cama.* por fah-BOHR seeEN-tehseh en la KAH-mah
Can you move over onto the bed?	*¿Puede moverse hacia la cama?* PWEH-deh moh-BERseh ahSEEah lah KAH-mah
I am going to take your temperature.	*Voy a tomarle la temperatura.* boy ah toh-MARleh lah tem-peh-rahTOOrah
Open your mouth.	*Abra la boca.* AH-brah lah BOH-kah

Lift up your tongue.	*Suba la lengua.* SOO-bah lah LEN-gwah
Keep your mouth closed.	*No abra la boca.* noh AH-brah lah BOH-kah
Please keep still.	*Por favor no se mueva.* pohr fah-BOHR noh seh MWEH-bah
Extend your arm.	*Extienda su brazo.* ekTEE-ENdah soo BRAH-soh
Roll up...please.	*Enrolle...por favor.* en-ROHjeh...pohr fab-BOHR
...your sleeves...	*...la manga...* lah MAHN-gah
...the sleeves of your blouse...	*...la manga de la blusa.* ...lah MAHN-gah deh lah BLOO-sah
Let me check your...	*Voy a verificar su...* boy ah beh-ree-feeKAR soo
...pulse.	*...pulso.* POOLsoh
...I.V.(intravenous)	*...intravenosa.* een-trah-behNOHsah
...vein.	*...vena.* BEHnah
This will be ...	*Esto será...* ES-toh sehRAH
...cold.	*...frío.* FREEoh
...hot.	*...caliente.* kah-LEE-ENteh
...hard.	*...duro.* DOOroh
...soft.	*...suave.* SWAHbeh

I am going to remove …	Voy a remover … boy ah reh-mohBER
…the bandage.	…la venda/curita. lah BENdah/koo-REEtah
…the dressing.	*…el vendaje.* el benDAH-heh
…these stitches.	*…estos puntos* EStos POON-tos
…the sutures.	*…las suturas.* las sooTOO-ras
Can I get you something for the pain?	*¿Podría tener algo para este dolor?* pohDREE-ah teh-NER ALgoh PAHrah ESteh doh-LOHR
These are for the pain.	*Estos son para el dolor.* EStos son PAH-rah el doh-LOHR
Take two of these.	*Tome dos de estos.* TOH-meh dos deh EStos
Are you allergic to any medication?	*¿Es usted alérgico a algún medicamento.* es oosTED ah-LERgee-koh ah ahl-GOON meh-dee-kahMENtoh
Are you still feeling pain?	*¿Toda vía le duele?* TOHdah BEEah leh DWEH-leh
All your test were negative.	*Todo el estudio es negativo* TOHdoh el es-TOOdee-oh es neh-gah-TEEboh
It is not serious.	*No es grave.* noh es GRAH-beh
Ask the doctor for the results of your tests.	*Pregunte al doctor por el resultado del estudio.* preh-GOONteh al doc-TOHR pohr el reh-soolTAH-doh del es-TOOdee-oh
I will get someone who speaks Spanish.	*Buscare alguien que hable español.* boosKAH-reh AHL-giehn keh AHB-leh es-pah-NYOL

You cannot…	*No puede …* noh PWEH-deh
…get out of bed today.	*…levantárse de la cama hoy* leh-ban-TARseh deh lah KAH-mah oi
…take a bath today.	*…bañarse hoy.* bah-NYARseh oi
Do not try to sit up.	*No tráte de levantárse.* noh TRAH-teh deh leh-banTAR-seh
You must…	*Tiene que …* teeEN-eh keh
…get out of bed today.	*…levantárse de la cama hoy.* leh-ban-TARseh deh lah KAH-mah oi
…try to sit up.	*…tratar de sentarse.* trah-TAHR deh senTAR-seh
…get up and walk today.	*…levantárse y caminar hoy.* leh-ban-TARseh ee kah-meeNAR oi
…sit in the chair today.	*…sentarse en la silla hoy.* sen-TAHRseh en lah SEEL-lah oi
You can only have a shower.	*Solo puedo ducharse.* SOH-loh PWEH-doh dooCHAR-seh
Do not bathe for …	*No se bañe por…* noh seh BAH-nyeh pohr
Do not take a bath until this wound heals.	*No se bañe hasta que la herida sane.* noh seh BAH-nyeh AHS-tah keh lah eh-REEdah SAH-neh
You are going to have an x-ray today.	*Va a tener unos rayos equis hoy.* bah ah tehn-NER OOnos RAH-jos EH-kees oi
You may get some bleeding for a few days.	*Tal vez va a sangrar por par de días.* tal bes vah ah sahn-GRAR por par dehDEE-as

Do not put anything into your vagina for...	*No ponga nada en su vagína por...* noh POHN-gah NAH-dah en soo bah-GEEnah por
no douche	*no ducha* noh DOO-chah
no sex	*no sexo* noh SEK-so
no tampons	*no tampones* noh tam-POHN-ehs
I need a sample your blood/stools/urine.	*Necesito una muestra de sangre/heces/orina.* neh-sehSEEtoh OOnah MWEHS-trah deh SAHN-greh/EH-sehs/ ohREEnah

POSSIBLE RESPONSES

I cannot eat/sleep.	*Yo no puedo comer/dormir.* joh noh PWEH-doh koh-MER/ dohr-MEER
I need sleeping pills.	*Necesito pildoras para dormir.* neh-sehSEEtoh peel-DOHras PAH-rah dohr-MEER
I am allergic to penicillin.	*Soy alégico a penisilina.* soy ah-LEHgee-koh ah peh-nee-seeLEEnah
It hurts here.	*Duele aquí.* DWEH-leh ah-KEE
I cannot turn	*No puedo virarme* noh PWEH-doh beeRAHR-meh
I cannot move	*No puedo mover.* noh PWEH-doh moh-BER
I cannot move...	*No puedo mover...* noh PWEH-doh moh-BER

...my neck.	*...mi cuello.* mee KWEH-joh
...my leg.	*...mi pierna.* mee PEE-ERnah
I cannot lift my leg.	*No puedo levantar mi pierna.* noh PWEH-doh leh-banTAR mee PEE-ERnah
Is it broken?	*¿Está rota?* esTAH ROH-tah
I need ...	*Necesito...* neh-seh-SEEtoh
...washbasin	*..una palangana.* OOnah pah-lan-GAHnah
...a bedpan	*...una silleta.* OOnah seel-LEHtah
I want to comb my hair.	*Quiero peinarme.* kee-EERoh pej-NARmeh
When can I get up?	*¿Cuándo puedo levantarme?* QWAN-doh PWEH-doh leh-ban-TARmeh
When can I go home?	*¿Cuándo puedo írme a casa?* QWAN-doh PWEH-doh EER-meh ahKAH-sah
What are the visiting hours?	*¿Cuáles son las horas de visita?* KWAH-les son las OH-ras de beeSEE-tah
Can I go home tomorrow?	*¿Puedo írme a casa mañana?* PWEH-doh EERmeh ah KAH-sah mah-NYAHnah
What time can the doctor come?	*¿A qué hora puede venir el doctor?* ah keh OH-rah PWEH-deh beh-NEER el doc-TOHR
I want to speak to the doctor.	*Quiero hablar con el doctor.* kee-EERoh ahb-LAR kon el doc-TOHR

I must call…

Tengo que llamar a…
TEN-goh keh jah-MAHR ah

…my husband/wife.

*…mi esposo/a**
mee esPOH-soh/sah

…my sister/brother.

…mi hermana/o
mee erMAH-nah/noh

**Use "o" for the masculine and "a" for the feminine.*

ADDRESSING THE PARENT/ GUARDIAN

Can you hold the baby while I take this test?	*¿Podria usted sostener el bebé mientras tomo este estudio?* poh-DREEah oosTED sos-TEHner elbeh-BEH meeEN-tras TOH-moh ES-teh es-TOOdee-oh
Hold the baby here.	*Aguante el bebé aquí.* ah-GWANteh el beh-BEH ah-KEE
Hold the baby like this (demonstrate)	*Aquante el bebé de esta manera* ah-GWANteh el beh-BEH deh es-TAH mah-NEHrah
Did anyone else come with you?	¿Alguien más vino con usted? AHL-giehn mas BEE-noh kon oosTED
...a relative?	*...un pariente?* ...oon pah-reeENteh
...a friend?	*...un amigo?* ...oon ah-MEEgoh
One of you will have to hold the baby during the test.	*Uno de ustedes tendrá que sostener el bebe mientras yo toma el estudio.* OOnoh deh oos-TEDes ten-DRAH keh sos-TEHner el beh-BEH meeENtras joh TOH-mah el es-TOOdee-o
Does the baby want ...	*¿Quiere el bebé...* kee-EHreh el beh-BEH
...his pacifier?	*...el bobo?* ...el BOH-boh
...his bottle?	*...la botella/ el biberón?* ...lah boh-TEHyah/ el bee-behRON
...a toy?	*...un juguete?* ...oon hoo-GEHteh

Is the baby hungry?	*¿Está el bebé con hambre?* es-TAH el beh-BEH kon AHMbreh
Did you feed him/her this morning?	*¿Le dio de comer esta mañana?* leh deeoh deh coh-MER ES-tah

ENGLISH-SPANISH DICTIONARY

Words are listed in alphabetical order regardless of whether the entry is one or two words.

Abbreviations:

v.	regular verb	*adj.*	adjective
*v.**	irregular conjugated verb	*adv.*	adverb
f.	feminine noun	*conj.*	conjunction
m.	masculine noun	*noun*	noun
pl.	plural	*prep.*	preposition
n.	numeral	*pron.*	pronoun
sing.	singular	*interr.*	interrogative

A

a	*un; una*
abdomen	*abdomen,m.*
able, be	*poder,v**
abnormal	*anormal,adj.*
abort	*abortar,v.*
abortion	*aborto,m.*
about(place)	*acerca de,prep.*
above	*sobre; encima de,prep.*
above	*arriba,adv.*
abscess	*abseso,m.*
absent	*ausente,adj.*
absolutely	*absolutamente, adv.*
absorb	*absorber,v**
abstain	*abstenerse,v**
abusive	*abusivo,adj.*
accept	*aceptar,v.*
accident	*accidente,m.*
accompany	*acompañar,v*
account(bill)	*cuenta,f.*
accurate	*correcto,adj.*
ache	*dolor,m.*
ache	*doler,v*.*
achieve	*conseguir,v**
acid	*acido,m.*
acquire	*obtener,v**
across	*por,prep.*
addict	*adicto/a, m./f.*
address	*dirección,f.*
adjust	*ajustar,v.*
administer	*aplicar,v**
advise(counsel)	*aconsejar,v.*
advise(inform)	*avisar,v.*
afraid	*miedoso,adj.*
afraid(to be)	*tener(v*) miedo*
after(position)	*detrás de,prep.*
after(time)	*después de,prep.*
afternoon	*tarde,f.*
afterwards	*después,adv.*
again	*otra vez,adv.*
against	*contra,prep.*
age	*edad,f.*
agree	*consentir,v**
ahead	*delante; al frente,adv.*
air	*aire,m.*
alcohol	*alcohol,m.*
all	*todo,adj.*
allergic	*alérgico,adv.*
allergy	*alergia,f.*
alone	*solo,adj.*
alone	*solamente,adv.*
along	*al lado de,prep.*
along with	*junto con*
also	*tambien,adv.*
always	*siempre,adv.*
almost	*casi,adv.*

among	*entre,prep.*
an	*un; una*
analgesic	*analgésico,m.*
anatomy	*anatomía,f.*
and	*y,conj.*
anemia	*anemia,f.*
anesthesia	*anestesia,f.*
anesthetic	*anestésico, m. & adj.*
ankle	*tobillo,m.*
anorexia	*anorexia,f.*
another	*otro,m., adj.,pron.*
anterior	*anterior,adj.*
antibiotic	*antibiótico, m.& adj.*
any	*alguno; algunos, adj.& pron.*
anybody	*alguien; alguno, pron.*
anything	*alguna cosa,pron.*
apart	*aparte,adj.*
apart	*separadamente, adv.*
appointment	*cita,f.*
approximate	*aproximado,adj.*
apron	*delantal,m.*
area	*área,f.*
arm	*brazo,m.*
arrive	*llegar,v**
artery	*arteria,f.*
artificial	*artificial,adj.*
as	*como; mientras; adv.,conj. & prep.*
ask	*preguntar,v.*
ask a question	*hacer(v*) una pregunta*
asleep	*dormido,adj.*
aspirin	*aspirina,f.*
as soon as	*tan pronto como*
asthma	*asma,f.*
asthmatic	*asmatico,adj.*
at	*a; en,prep.*
August	*agosto,m.*
aunt	*tia,f.*
autopsy	*autopsia,f.*
autumn	*otoño,m.*
away	*lejos,adv.*

B

baby	*bebé,f./m.*
back	*espalda,f.*
backbone	*espinazo,m.,*
backwards	*hacia atrás; para atrás, adv.*
bag	*cartera,f; bolso/a,m./f.*
bandage	*curita,f; venda,f.*
bandaging	*vendaje,f.*
bar(rod)	*barra,f.*
bath	*baño,m.*
bathroom	*cuarto de baño,m.*
be(permanent)	*ser,v**
be(temporary)	*estar,v**
because	*porque,conj.*
because of	*por*
bed	*cama,f.*
bedpan	*sillet,f; cómodo,f.*
before	*antes de;delante de; enfrente de, adv.*
begin	*comenzar,v*; empezar,v*.*
behave yourself	*¡portate bien!*
behind	*atrás,adv.*
believe	*creer,v*.*
belly	*vientre,m.*
below	*abajo; debajo, adv.*
belt	*correa,f; cinto,m.*
bend	*doblar(se), v*
beneath	*debajo de,prep.*
beret	*boina,f.*
beside	*cerca de, prep.*
between	*entre,prep.*
big	*grande, adj.*
billing dept.	*departamento de cobro,m.*
birth	*nacimiento,m.*
black	*negro, adj.*
bladder	*vejiga,f.*
blanket	*mante,f.*
bleed	*sangrar,v.*
blind	*ciego,adj.*
blood	*sangre,f.*
blood pressure	*presión sanguínea,f.*
blood transfusion	*transfusión de sangre,f.*
blood vessel	*vaso sanguíneo,m.*

blouse *blusa,f; camisa,f.*
blue *azul, adj.*
body *cuerpo,m.*
bone *huesp,m.*
book *libro,m.*
boot *bota,f.*
both *ambos,adj. & pron.*
bottle(baby) *botella,f; biberon,m.*
bottom *fondo,m.*
bowels *intestino, mpl.*
boy *niño,m; chico,m.*
bracelet *brazalete,m.*
brain *cerebro,m.*
brassiere *sostén,m.*
breakfast *desyuno,m.*
breast *seno,m.*
breath *respiro,m.*
breathe *respirar,v.*
breathing *respiración,f.*
bring *llevar,v*
brother *hermano,m.*
brown *moreno; café, adj.*
burn *quemadura,f.*
burn *quemar,v*
business *ocupación,f; trabajo,m.*
busy *ocupado,adv.*
but *pero, conj., prep. & adv.*
buttock *nalga,m.*
button *botón,m.*
by *por,prep.*
by (near) *cerca de, adv.*

C

cafe *café, m.*
cafeteria *restaurante,m.*
call(only phone) *llamar(v*) por teléfono*
calm *calma,f.*
calm *calmar,v.*
calm down *calmar(se) v; aquietarse,v.*
cancel *cancelar,v.*
cancer *cáncer,m.*
candy *dulce,m.; bombón,m.*
cane (for walking) *bastón,m.*
cap *gorro,m.*
capillary *capilar,adj.*
car *coche,m.; auto,m.*
card *tarjeta,f.*
care *cuidado,m.*
career *profesión,f.*
careful(to be) *tener(v*) cuidado*
carry *llevar,v.*
cashier *cajero,m.; caja,f.*
cataract *catarata,f.*
cause *causa,f.*
cavity(tooth) *carie,f.*
center *centro,m.*
cervix *cerviz,f.*
chain *cadena,f.*
chair *silla,f.*
check(bank) *cheque,m.*
cheek *mejilla,f.*
chest *pecho,m.*
chewing gum *chicle,m; goma de mascar,f.*
child *niño/a,m./f.; hijo/a,m./f.*
childbirth *parto,m; alumbramiento,m.*
chin *barba,f.; mentón,m.*
chin (the point of) *barbilla,f.*
choice *selección,f.*
to have no other choice *no tener(v*) otra alternativa*
choke *sofocar,v*.*
cigar *puro,m.*
cigarette *cigarrillo,m.*
city *ciudad,f.*
clean *limpio,adj.*
clear *claro,adj.*
clergyman *clérigo,m.; pastor,m.*
clinic *clínica,f*
clock *reloj,m.*
close *próximo,adj.*
close(near) *proximo,adj.*
cloth *tela,f.*

clothes	*ropa,f.*
coffee	*café,m.*
coffee shop	*tienda de café,m.*
cold	*frío,adj.*
cold(illness)	*catarro,m.*
colic	*cólico,m.*
colon	*colon,m.*
color	*color,m.*
coma	*coma,f.*
comb	*peine,m.*
come	*venir,v*; llegar,v*.*
come back	*regresar,v.*
come down	*bajar,v.*
come in	*entrar,v.*
come out	*salir,v*.*
come off	*soltarse,v*.*
come up	*subir,v.*
comfortable	*comfortable, adj.*
compare	*comparar,v.*
complete	*completo, adj.*
complete	*completar,v.*
complexion	*cutis,m. tez,f.*
complicated	*complicado,adj.*
compress	*apretar,v*; condensar,v.*
computer	*computadora,f.*
concussion	*concusión,f.*
conference	*consulta,f.*
confuse	*confundir,v.*
confused	*confuso,adj.*
connect	*conectar,v.*
conscious	*consciente,adj.*
consent	*consentimiento,m.*
consent	*consentir,v**
constipate	*estreñir,v**
constipation	*estreñimiento,m.*
consult	*consultar,v.*
contact lens	*lentes de contacto, mpl; letillas,fpl.*
continue	*continuar,v*.*
continuous	*continuo,adj.*
cooperation	*cooperación,f.*
copy	*copia,f.*
corduroy	*pana,f.*
corpse	*cadaver,m.*
correct	*correcto,adj.*
correct	*corregir,v*.*
it is correct	*está bien*
correctly	*correctamente,adv.*
cotton	*algodón,m.*
cough	*tos,f; catarro,m.*
cough	*toser,v.*
cousin	*primo/a,m./f.*
cranium	*cráneo,m.*
critical	*crítico,adj.*
crowd	*pueblo,m.*
cry	*grito,m.*
cry	*gritar,v.*
cup	*taza,m.*
cut	*corte,m.*

D

dad	*papá,m.*
daily	*diario,adj.*
danger	*peligro,m.*
dangerous	*peligroso,adj.*
dark	*obscuro,adj.*
date	*fecha,f.*
daughter	*hija,f.*
day	día,f.
dead	*muerto,adj.*
deaf	*sordo,adj.*
death	*muerte,f.*
December	*diciembre,m.*
deep	*profundo,adj.*
dentist	*dentista,f.*
denture	*dentadura postiza,f.*
deodorant	*desodorante,m.*
department	*departamento,m.*
diagnose	*diagnosticar,v**
diaper	*pañal,m.*
diarrhea	*diarrea,f.*
die	*morir(se), v*.*
difficult	*dificil,adj.*
difficultly	*dificultad,f.*
digest	*digerir,v**
digestion	*digestión,f.*
digestive tract	*canal digestivo,m.*
dilute	*diluir,v*.*
dim	*obscuro,adj.*
dinner	*comida,f.*
direction	*dirección,f.*
dirty	*sucio,adj.*
discharge	*secretión,f.*
disease	*enfermedad,f.*

disinfectant *desinfectante,m.*
disinfectant *desinfectar,v.*
divorce *divorcio,m.*
dizzy *mareado,adj.*
do *hacer,v**
doctor *doctor,m; médico,m.*
doll *muñeca,f.*
dollar *dólar,m.*
door *puerta,f.*
doorknob *tirador de puerta, f.*
dorsal spine *espina dorsal,f.*
doorway *entrada,f.*
douche *ducha vaginal,f.*
down *abajo; hacia abajo,adv.*
dress *vestidura,f.*
dress *vestir(se),v*.*
dressing (bandage) *bendage,m.*
drink *beber,v.*
drive (a car) *guiar,v**
drowsy *soñoliento, adj.*
drug *droga,f.*
drug addict *drogadicto,m.*
drugstore *farmacia,f.*
drunk(to get) *emborracharse,v.*
dry *seco,adj.*
dull paindolor *sordo,m.*
during *durante,prep.*

E

each *cada,adj.*
ear *oreja,f.*
early *temprano,adj.*
earring *pantalla,f; pendiente,m.*
easy *fácil,adj.*
eat *comer,v.*
eat breakfast *desayunarse,v; tomar(v.) el desaynno*
eat diner *tomar(v.) la comida*
edge *borde,m.*
eight *ocho,n.*
eighteen *dieciocho,n.*
eighty *ochenta,n.*
either *uno u otro,pron.*
either of the two *cualquiera de los dos*
elbow *codo,m.*
elderly *viejo,adj.*
elevator *ascensor,m; elevador,m.*
eleven *once,n.*
else *otro,adj. & adv.*
elsewhere *en otro parte,adv.*
emergency *emergencia,f.*
emphysema *enfisema,f.*
employee *empleado,m.*
employer *patrón,m.*
employment *ocupación,f.*
empty *vacío,adj.*
end *terminar,v.*
enema *enema,f.*
English *inglés,adj.*
enough *bastante,adv.*
enter *entrar,v.*
entire *todo,adj.*
entrance *entrada,f.*
envelope *sobre,m.*
epidemic *epidemia,f.*
equal *igual,adj.*
equipment *equipo,m.*
evacuate *evacuar,v.*
evening *tarde,f.*
ever *siempre,adv.*
every *cada,adj.*
every other day *cada dos días*
everybody *todos; todo el mundo,pron.*
everyday *cada día,adj.*
everyone *todos; cada uno,pron.*
everything *todo,pron.*
everywhere *por; en, adv.*
exacto exacto,adj.
examination *exámen,m; estudio,m.*
examine *examinar,v.*
except *excepto; menos,prep.*
excuse *excusa,f.*
excuse *excusar,v.*
exit *salida,f.*

expect	*aguarder,v.*
expensive	*costoso,adj.*
expert	*experto,m.*
expire	*expirar,v.*
explain	*explicar,v.*
eye	*ojo,m.*
eyeball	*globo del ojo,m.*
eyebrow	*ceja,f.*
eyeglass	*lente,m.*
eyelash	*pestaña,f.*
eyelid	*párpado,m.*
eye sight	*vista,f.*

F

fabric	*género,m.*
face	*cara,f.*
facial tissue	*papel facial,m.*
faint	*débil,adj.*
faint	*desmayarse,v.*
faint	*desmayo,m.*
fall	*caída,f.*
fall	*caer,v*.*
fall asleep	*dormir(se),v*.*
family	*familia,f.*
family name	*apellido,m.*
far	*lejos,adj.*
fast	*rápido,adj*
fasten	*fijar,v.*
fat	*gordo,adj.*
father	*padre,m.*
father-in-law	*suegro,m.*
faucet	*grifo,m.*
February	*febrero,m.*
feed	*dar(v.*) de comer*
feel	*sentir,**
feet	*pie,m.*
female	*hembra,f.*
femur	*fémur,m.*
fetus	*feto,m.*
fever	*fiebre,f.*
feverish	*febril,adj.*
few	*pocos,adj.*
fifteen	*quince,n.*
fifty	*cincuenta,n.*
fight	*lucha,f.*
fight	*lunchar,v.*
fill	*llenar,v.*
final	*final,adj.*
find	*encontrar,v*.*
fine	*perfecto,adj.*
finger	*dedo (de la mano),m.*
fingernail	*uña,f.*
finish	*fin,m; término,m.*
finish	*terminar,v.*
fire	*fuego,m.*
first	*primero,adj.*
first aid	*primeros auxilios, m.pl.*
first floor	*primer piso.*
fist	*puño,m.*
five	*cinco,n.*
fix	*remendar,v*; ajustar,v.*
floor	*suelo,m.piso,m.*
flow	*flujo,m.*
flow	*fluir,v*.*
flu	*gripe,f; influenza,f.*
fluids	*fluídos,m.pl.*
fluctuate	*fluctuar,v*.*
fold (double over)	*doblar,v.*
follow	*seguir,v**
food	*comida,f.*
foot	*pie,m.*
footstool	*banquillo,m.*
for	*por; para,prep.*
forearm	*antebrazo,m.*
forehead	*frente,f.*
forget	*olvidar,v.*
forgive	*perdoner,v.*
form	*forma,f.*
forty	*cuarenta,n.*
four	*cuatro ,n.*
fourteen	*catorce,n.*
forth	*cuatro,n.*
forward	*hacia adelante; hacia el frente,adv.*
free(no fee)	*gratis,adj.*
Friday	*viernes,m.*
friend	*amigo,m.*
from	*de,prep.*
front	*frente,m.*
front of	*delante de*
full	*lleno; completo,adj.*

G

gallbladder *vesícula (biliar),f; vejiga de la hiel,f.*
gallstones *cálculo biliar,m.*
gap *abertura,f.*
gargle *gárgarear,v.*
gastric *gástrico,adj.*
gastrointestinal *gastrointestinal,adj.*
gate *entrada,f.*
gauze *gasa,f.*
gay *homosexual,adj.*
gentle *cuidadoso; suave,adj.*
germ *germen microbío,m.*
get *obtener,v**
get down *bajar,v.*
get on *subir(v.) a*
get out *salir,v**
get up *levantarse,v.*
girl *niña,f.*
give *dar,v**
glad *contento,adj.*
glad(to be) *alegrarse(v.) de*
gland *glándula.f.*
glass(container) *vaso,m.*
glass(for eye) *lentes,m; espejuelos,m.*
glove *guante,m.*
go *ir(se),v**
god *dios,m.*
go out *salir,v**
goiter *bocio,m.*
gold *oro,m.*
good *bueno,adj.*
good afternoon *buenos tardes*
good day/ morning *buenos días*
good night *buenos noches*
good bye *adios*
gown (hospital's) *bata,f.*
grand child *nieto/a, m./f.*
grand children *nietos,mpl.*
granddaughter *nieta,f.*
grandson *nieto,m.*
grandfather *abuelo,m; papá grande,m.*
grandmother *abuela,m; mamá grande,f.*
green *verde,adj.*
grey *gray,adj.*
gum (glue) *goma,f.*
gum (chewing) *chicle,m.*

H

hair *pelo,m.*
hairbrush *cepillo para el cabello,m.*
hair pin *gancho para el pelo,m.*
half hour *media hora,f.*
hand *mano,f.*
handbag *bolso/a, m./f.*
handbag *cartera,f.*
hardly ever *casi nunca*
hat *sombrero,m.*
have *tener,v*; haber,v**
he *el,pron.*
head *cabeza,f.*
head ache *dolor de cabeza,m.*
heal *curar,v; sanar,v.*
health insurance *seguro médico,m.*
hear *oír,v**
heart *corazón,m.*
heart attack *ataque al corazón,m.*
heart rate *velocidad del corazón,m.*
heart trouble *enfermedad de corazón,m.*
heat *calor,m.*
heel *talón del pie,m.*
height *altura,f.*
help *ayuda,f.*
hemoglobin *hemoglobina,f.*
hemorrhage *hemorragia,f.*
hemorrhoids *hemorroides,f.*
hepatitis *hepatitis,f.*
here *aquí; acá,adv.*
hereditary *hereditario,adj*
high *alto,adj.*
hip *cadera,f.*
hit *pegar,v.*
hold *aguantar,v.*
hold *tener(se),v*; sostener,v*.*

hold on	*agarrarse,v.*
hold up	*levantar,v.*
holiday	*día de fiesta,m; día festivo,m.*
home	*casa,f.*
homosexual	*homosexual,adj.*
hospital	*hospital,m.*
hour	*hora,f.*
how	*cómo,adv./adj.*
how	*qué,interr.*
how long	*cuánto tiempo*
how much/ many	*cuántos*
how soon?	*¿cuándo?*
hug	*abrazar,v**
hundred	*cien(to),n.*
hunger	*hambre,f.*
hungry(to be)	*tener(v*.) hambre*
hurry	*apresurar(se),v.*
to be in a hurry	*tener(v*) prisa*
hurry up	*apresurar(se),v*; ar(se)(v*.) prisa*
hurt	*hacer(v*) daño, dañar,v.*
husband	*marido,m. esposo,m.*

I

I	*yo,pron.*
ice	*hielo,m.*
ice chips	*hielo,m.*
identification	*identificación,f.*
if	*si,adv.*
ill	*enfermo; malo,adj.*
ill(to become)	*enfermar,v.*
image	*imagen,f.*
immediate	*inmediato,adj.*
immediately	*inmediatemente,adv.*
implant	*implantar,v.*
important	*importante,adj.*
in	*en; dentro de,prep.*
in front of	*frente a*
incision	*incisión,f.*
infant	*bebé,m.*
infect	*infectar,v.*
infected	
(to become)	*infectarse,v.*
infection	*infección,f; contagio,m.*
inflate	*inflar,v.*
influenza	*gripe,f.*
information	*información,f.*
inhale	*inspirar,v.*
inject	*inyectar,v.*
injected	*inyectado*
injection	*inyección,f.*
insane	*insano,m. loco,m.*
insert	*insertar,v.*
inside	*dentro,adv./adj.*
insist	*insistir(v.) en*
inspect	*examinar,v.*
instruct	*instruir,v*.*
instruction	*instrucción,f.*
insulin	*insulina,f.*
insurance	*seguro,m.*
insurance policy	*póliza de seguro,f.*
intense	*intenso,adj.*
interpret	*interpretar,v.*
intestine	*intestino,m.*
into	*en; dentro de, prep./adv.*
intoxicate	*intoxicar,v**
intravenous	*intravenoso,adj.*
invalid	*inválido; enfermizo,adj.*
iodine	*yodo,m.*
iris(of eyes)	*iris,m;*
I.V.	*suero ó intravenosa,m.*

J

jacket	*chaqueta,f.*
jaw	*quijada,f; mandíbula,f.*
jersey	*jersey,f; blusa,f.*
jewelry	*prenda,f; joya,f.*
job	*trabajo,m; ocupación,f.*
join	juntar,v.
joint	*articulación,f.*
juice	*jugo,m.*
July	*julio,m.*
June	*junio,m.*

K

keep *retener, v*.*
key *llave,f.*
keyring *llavero,m.*
kidney *riñon,m.*
kidney stones *cálculos,m.*
kidney stones *piedra en el riñon,f.*
knee *rodilla,f.*
knife *cuchillo,m.*
knock *golpear,v.*
knock on the door *llamar(v.) a la puerta*
knock kneed *patizambo,adj.*
know (acquainted) *conocer, v**
know (knowledge) *saber, v*.*

L

labor(to be in) *estar(v*.) de parto*
lady *señora,f; dama,f.*
laryngitis *laringitis,adj.*
larynx *laringe,f.*
last *último; final,adj.*
last name *apellido,m.*
last night *anoche*
late *tardo,adj.*
late(to be) *ser(v*.) tarde*
lateral *lateral,adj.*
lavatory *lavatorio,m.*
lay *colocar,v*.*
lead *plomo,m.*
learn *aprender,v.*
least *menos,adj.pron.*
leather *cuero,adj.*
leave *dejar,v.*
left *izquierdo,adj.*
left(hand/side) *izquierda,f.*
leg *pierna,f.*
lens *lentes,mpl*
lesion *lesión,f.*
less *menos,adv*
let go *soltar,v*.*
lie *acostarse,v**
lie back *recostarse,v; echarse(v.) hacia atrás*
lift *levantar,v.*
like *como,adv.*
lip *labio,m.*
lipstick *lápiz(m.) para los labios*
liquid *líquido,m.*
listen *escuchar,v*
little *pequeño; poco,adj.*
little finger *dedo meñique,m.*
liver *hígado,m.*
lobe *lóbulo,m.*
locate *localizar,v*.*
location *situación,f.*
lock(door) *cerradura,f.*
locker *armario,m.*
long *largo,adj.*
long ago *hace mucho tiempo*
how long is it since *cuánto tiempo hace que*
look *mirar,v.*
look for *buscar,v*.*
look into *examinar,v.*
look up *levantar(v.) la vista*
loose(slack) *suelto,adj.*
loose(to come) *soltarse,v*.*
lose consciousness *perder(v*.) el sentido*
loosen *soltar,v*.*
lose *perder,v*.*
lubricant *lubricante,adj.*
lubricate *lubricar,v*.*
lubrication *lubricación,f.*
lump *masa,f. bolsa,f.*
lunch *almuerzo,m.*
lunch(to have) *tomar(v.) almuerzo*
lung *pulmón,m.*
lymph *linfa,f.*

M

machine *máquina,f.*
magnet *iman,m*
magnetic *magnético,adj.*

Magnetic Resonance Imaging	*Resonancia magnética,f.*
magnify	*amplificar, v*.*
maintain	*mantener, v*.*
make	*hacer, v**
malignant	*maligno, adj.*
malnutrition	*desnutrición,f.*
mama	*mamá,f.*
man	*hombre, m.*
man and wife	*marido (m.) y mujer (f.)*
manager	*director, m.*
manner(way)	*manera,f.*
manslaughter	*homicidio, m.*
many	*muchos, adj.*
March	*marzo, m.*
mark	*marca,f.*
mark	*marcar, v**
married	*casado, adj.*
marry	*casar, v.*
mass	*masa,f.*
maternity	*maternidad,f.*
May	*mayo, m.*
maybe	*quizás; tal vaz, adv.*
me	*me; mí, pron.*
meal	*comida,f.*
measles	*sarampión, m.*
medical	*médico, m.*
medical insurance	*seguro médico, m.*
medication	*medicacion,f.*
medicine	*medicina,f; medicamento, m.*
meet	*encontrar (se), v*.*
membrane	*menbrana,f.*
memory	*memoria,f.*
menstruation	*menstruo, m; menstrua1ción,f.*
mental	*mental, adj.*
metabolism	*metabolismo, m.*
metal	*metal, m.*
metallic	*metálico, adj.*
microscope	*microscopio, m.*
midday	*mediodía, m.*
middle	*medio, m.*
middle finger	*dedo del corazón, m.*
milk	*leche,f.*
million	*millón, n.*
mine	*mío, pron.*
minister	*ministro, m; pastor, m.*
minor	*menor de edad, adj.*
minute	*minuto, m.*
miscarriage	*aborto, m; malparto, m.*
Miss	*señorita,f.*
mistake	*error, m.*
mistake	*equívoco, adj.*
mistaken	*equivocado, adj.*
mix	*mezclar (se), v*.*
mixture	*equívoco, m.*
Monday	*lunes, m.*
money	*dinero, m.*
month	*mes, m.*
more	*más, adj.*
morning	*mañana,f.*
morphine	*morfina,f.*
most	*casi, adv.*
mother	*madre,f.*
mouth	*boca,f.*
move	*mover (se), v**
Mr.	*señor, m.*
much	*mucho, adj.*
mucous	*mucoso, adj.*
mucous membrane	*membrana mucosa,f.*
mumps	*paperas,fpl;parótidas,fpl.*
murmur	*murmullo, m.*
muscle	*músculo, m.*
my	*mi*

N

naked	*desnudo, adj.*
name	*nombre, m.*
nasal	*nasal, adj.*
nausea	*náusea,f.*
navel	*ombligo, m.*
near	*cerca, adv.*
neck	*nuca,f; cuello, m.*
necklace	*collar, m.*
necktie	*corbata,f.*
nerve	*nervio, m.*
nervous	*nervioso, adj.*
nervous breakdown	*crisis nerviosa,f.*

neurotic *neurótico,m.*
never *nunca; jamais,adv.*
never mind *no importa*
newspaper *periódico,m.*
next *próximo,m.*
next to *junto a; al lado; después de*
niece *sobrina,f.*
night *noche,f.*
nine *nueve,n.*
nineteen *diecinueve,n.*
ninety *noventa,n.*
nipple *pezón,m.*
no *no,adv.*
nobody *nadie; ninguno,pron.*
nobody else *ningun otro*
nod *inclinar(v.) la cabeza*
noise *ruido,m.*
none *ningumo; nada,pron./adj.*
noon *mediodía,m.*
nor *ni...ni,conj./adv.*
normal *normal,adj.*
nose *nariz,f.*
nostrils *ventanas de la nariz,fpl.*
not *no,adv.*
note *nota,f. apunte,m.*
nothing *nada,pron.*
nothing else *nada más*
November *noviembre,m.*
now *ahora,adv.*
nuclear *nuclear,adj.*
numb *entumecido,adj.*
number *número,m.*
nun *monja,f.*
nurse *enfermera,f.*

O

obey *obedecer,v*.*
o'clock *de*
occupation *ocupación,f.*
October *octubre,m.*
of *de,prep.*
off (distance) *lejos,adv.*
off (not attached) *suelto,adv.*
office *oficina,f.*
often *muchas veces,adv.*
O.K. *bueno,adj.*
old *viejo,m.*
olfactory *olfatorio,adj.*
on *en; a; sobre; encima de,prep.*
once *una vez,adv.*
one *un; uno,adj.*
only *solo; solamente,adj.*
onto *a; sobre,prep.*
opaque *opaco,adj.*
open *abrir,v*.*
opening *abertura,f.*
operate *operar,v.*
operation *operación,f.*
optic *óptico,adj.*
optical *óptico,adj.*
optician *óptico,m.*
or *o; u(before -o- or -ho-)*
oral *oral,adj.*
orange *naranja,f.*
orbit *órbita,f.*
order(request) *order,m.*
organ *órgano,m.*
other *otro,m./adj*
outside *fuera de,prep; afuera,adv.*
ovary *ovarío,m.*
over *sobre; por encima de,prep.*
overcoat *abrigo,m.*
owe *deber,v; adeudar,v.*
oxygen *oxígeno,m.*

P

pacemaker *marcapaso,m.*
pacifier(baby) *bobo,m; chupete,m.*
pain *dolor,m.*
painful *doloroso,adj.*

painkiller *analgésico,m.*
painless *sin dolor; libre de dolor,adj.*
pajamas *pijama,f.*
palate *paladar,m.*
pale *pálido,m.*
palpitate *palpitar,v.*
pants *pantalón,m.*
papa *papá,m.*
paper *papel,m.*
paper tissue *papel de seda,m.*
paralysis *parálisis,f.*
paralyze *paralizar,v*.*
pardon *perdón,m.*
parent *padre,m; madre,f.*
past *pasado,m.*
pastor *pastor,m; clérigo,m.*
pathology *patología,f.*
patient *paciente,m; enfermo,m.*
pay *pagar,v*.*
pay attention *atender,v*.*
payment *pago,m.*
payment in full *pago total*
pelvis *pelvis,f.*
pen *pluma,f.*
pencil *lápiz,m.*
penis *pene,m.*
penicillin *peninsulína,f.*
people *gente,f.*
period (menstrual) *periodo,m.*
phalanx *falanje,f.*
pharmacist *farmacéutico,adj.*
pharmacy *farmacia,f.*
pharynx *faringe,f.*
phone *teléfono,m.*
photo *fotografía,f.*
photographic plate *placa,f.*
picture *fotografía,f.*
pill *píldora,f.*
pillow *almohada,f.*
pillowcase *prenda de almohada,f.*
pin(safety pin) *imperdible,*m.
plasma *plasma,m.*
plaster of Paris *yeso,m.*
plastic *plástico,m.*
please *agradar,v.*
pneumonia *pulmonía,f.*
pocket *bolsillo,m.*
pocket book *bolsa,f.*
pocket knife *navaja,f.*
point *punto,m.*
poison *veneno,m; ponzoña,f.*
police *policía,f./m.*
poor *pobre,adj.*
portable *portátil,adj.*
powder *polvo,m.*
pregnant *embarazada,adj.*
preliminary *preliminar,adj./m.*
prenatal *prenatal,adj.*
preparation *preparación,f.*
prescribe *prescriber,v*; recetar,v.*
prescription *prescripción,f; receta,f.*
previous *anterior; anteriormente,adj.*
prior *previo,m.*
private *privado,m.*
problem *problema,f.*
prone *propenso,adj.*
prostate *próstata,f.*
psychiatrist *siquiatra,f.*
psychiatry *siquiatría,f.*
psychologist *sicologo,m.*
psychology *sicología,f.*
public *público,adj./m.*
pull *jalar,v.*
purpose *propósito,m; intención,f.*
pus *podre,f; pus,m.*
pulse *pulso,m.*
push *empujar,v; pujar,v.*
put *poner,v*.*

Q

question *pregunta,f.*
questionnaire *cuestionario,m; lista de preguntas,f.*

quick	*pronto; rápido,adj.*
quiet	*quieto,adj.*
quiet(to be)	*tapar(v.) la boca; callar,v.*

R

radiation	*radioción,f.*
radioactive	*radiactivo,adj.*
radiograph	*radiografía,f.*
radiology	*radiología,f.*
rape	*violación,f.*
rape	*violar,v.*
rapid	*rápido,adj.*
rash(on skin)	*erupcíon,f. salpullido,m.*
ray	*rayo,m.*
reach	*llegar,v*.*
read	*leer,v*.*
reason	*razón,f; causa,f.*
receipt	*recibo,m.*
rectum	*recto,m.*
red	*rojo,adj.*
refund	*reembolso,m.*
refund	*reembolsar,v.*
refuse	*rehusar,v.*
regulate	*regular,v.*
reimburse	*reembolsar,v.*
related	*relatado,adj.*
we are related	*somos parientes; estamosem parentados*
relative	*pariente,m./f.*
relax	*relajar,v; tranquilizar,v*.*
release	*soltar,v*.*
remain	*quedarse,v.*
remove	*quiter,v.*
repair	*reparar,v.*
request	*orden,f.*
requisition	*requisición,f.*
respiration	*respiración,f.*
result	*resulta,f; resultado,m.*
return	*regresar,v.*
rheumatism	*reumatismo,m.*
rib	*costilla,f.*
right	*derecho,adj.*
right (hand/side)	*derecha,f.*
ring (for finger)	*sortija,f.*
ring finger	*dedo anular,m.*
roll	*rodar,v*.*
room	*cuarto,m;*
room(large)	*sala,f.*
routine	*rutina,adj.*
rub (with alcohol)	*fricción con alcohol,f.*

S

safe	*seguro ,adj.*
safety-pin	*imperdible,m.*
sag	*combarse,v.*
saline	*salino,adj.*
saliva	*saliva,f.*
same	*mismo; idéntico,adj.*
sample	*muestra,f.*
sanitary	*sanitario,adj.*
sanitary napkins	*toalla sanitaria,f.*
Saturday	*sábado,m.*
say	*decir,v*.*
scale	*escala,f.*
scalp	*cuero,m.*
scar(on skin)	*cicatríz,f.*
scarf	*bufanda,f; mantilla,f.*
school	*escuela,f.*
scissors	*tijeras,fpl.*
search	*buscar,v**
second	*segundo,adj.*
secretary	*secretario,m./f.*
secrete	*secretar,v.*
secretion	*secreción,f.*
security	*seguridad,f.*
sedation	*sedación,f.*
sedative	*sedativo,m; calmante,m.*
see	ver,v*.
send	*enviar,v*.*
senile	*senil,adj.*
sensitive	*sensitivo,adj.*
separate	*separado,adj.*

September	*septiembre,m.*
seven	*siete,n.*
seventeen	*diecisiete,n.*
seventy	*setenta,n.*
sex	*sexo,m.*
shake	*menear(se),v.*
sharp(pain)	*intenso,adj.*
shave	*afeitar(se),v.*
sheet	*sábana,f.*
shin	*espinilla,f.*
shirt	*camisa,f.*
shoe	*zapato,m.*
shoelace	*gabete,m; lazo,m.*
shop	*tienda,f.*
short (length of clothing)	*cordo,adj.*
short (height)	*bajo,adj.*
shoulder	*hombro,m.*
shout	*gritar,v.*
shut	*cerrar(se),v*.*
sick	*enfermo; malo,adj.*
sickle	*hoz,f.*
side	*lado,m.*
signature	*firma,f.*
silk	*seda,adj.*
silver	*plata,f.*
since	*desde que; depués (de) que, conj.*
sinus	*sinus,f; cavidad (en un hueso),f.*
sinusitis	*sinusítis,f.*
sip	*sorber,v; chupar,v.*
sir	*señor,m.*
sister	*hermana,f.*
sit	*sentar,v*.*
sit down	*sentarse,v*.*
six	*seis,n.*
sixteen	*dieciséis,n.*
sixty	*sesenta,n.*
skeleton	*esqueleto,m.*
skin	*piel,f; curtis,m.*
skirt	*falda,f.*
skull	*cráneo,m.*
sleep	*sueño,m.*
sleep (to go to)	*dormir(se),v*.*

slipper	*zapatilla,f.*
slow	*lento,adj*
slowly	*despacio,adv.*
small	pequeño,adj.
smaller	menor,adj.
smallpox	*viruela,f.*
smart	*listo,adj.*
smell	*oler,v*.*
smoke	*fumar,v.*
sneeze	*éstornudo,m.*
sneeze	*éstornuder,v.*
snore	*ronquido,m.*
snore	*roncar,v.*
so	*muy,adv.*
soak	*remojar,v.*
soap	*jabón,m.*
social security	*seguro social,m; seguridad,f.*
sock	*media,f.*
socket(of eye)	*cuenca del ojo,f.*
soda	*soda,f.*
soft	*tierno; dulce,adj.*
sole of foot	*planta del pie,f.*
solid	*sólido,adj./m.*
solution	*solución,f.*
some	*algún; algunos,adj.*
someone	*alguien; alguno,pron.*
somebody	*alguien,pron.*
somebody else	algún otro
something	*algo; alguna cosa, pron.*
sometime	*algún día; alguna vez,adv.*
somewhere	*en alguna parte,adv.*
somewhere else	*en alguna otra parte*
so much	*tanto*
son	*hijo,m.*
soon	*pronto,adv; presto,adv.*
as soon as	*tan pronto como*
how soon?	*¿cuándo?*
sore	*dolorido,adv.*
to have a sore throat	*tener(v*.) mal de garganta*
Spanish	*español,m.*
speak	*hablar,v.*

special *especial,adj.*
specimen *espécimen,m.*
speedy *rápido,adj.*
sperm *esperma,f.*
spill *verter,v*.*
spinal *espinal,adj.*
spine *espina,f.*
spleen *bazo,m.*
sponge *esponja,f.*
spoon *cuchara,f.*
spoonful *cucharada,f.*
spouse *esposo,m.*
squeeze *apretar,v*.*
stair *escalón,m.*
staircase *escalera,f.*
stand *pararse,v.*
stand aside *apartarse,v.*
stand back of *colocarse(v*.) detras de*
stand up *poner(v*.) de pie; poner(v*.) derecho*
start *comenzar,v*.*
starve *morir(se),v*.*
starving *hambriento,adj.*
State *Estado,m.*
stay *quedar(se),v.*
steam *vapor,m.*
step(stairs) *pisada,f.*
step aside *hacerse(v*.) a un lado*
step down *bajar,v.*
step out *salír,v.*
step up *subír,v.*
sterilize *esterilizar,v*.*
stethoscope *estetoscopio,m.*
still *quieto,adj.*
still(to be) *aquietar,v; calmar,v.*
stir *menear,v.*
stomach *estómago,m.*
stool (excrement) *excremento,m.*
stool (furniture) *escalón,m.*
stop *parar(se),v.*
store *tienda,f.*
straight *derecho; recto,adj.*
strap(belt) *correa,f.*
street *calle,f.*
stretcher *camilla,f.*
string *cuerda,f.*
stroke *ataque,m.*
strong *fuerte,adj.*
student *estudiante,m./f.*
study *estudio,m.*
study *estudiar,v.*
sue *demandar,v.*
suffocation *asfíxia,f; sofoco,m.*
sugar *azúcar,f.*
sulphate *sulfato,m.*
summer *verano,m.*
Sunday *domingo,m.*
super *cena,f.*
supervisor *superintendente,m.*
support *mantener,v*.*
sure *seguro,adj.*
surface *superficie,f.*
surgeon *cirujano,m.*
surgery *operación,f; cirujía,f.*
surgical *quirúrgico,adj.*
surname *apellido,m.*
sutures *suturas,f.pl.*
swallow *tragar,v*.*
sweet *dulce,m.*
swell *hinchar,v.*
swollen *hindarse,v.*
synthetic *sintético,adj.*
syringe *jeringa,f.*

T

table *mesa,f.*
tablespoon *cuchara,f.*
tablespoonful *cucharada,f.*
take *tomar,v.*
take off *quitar,v.*
take out *sacar,v*.*
talk *hablar,v.*
tall *alto,adj.*
tampon *tampon,m.*
tap(faucet) *llave,f.*
tap (hit) *tocar,v*.*
tape(adhesive) *adhesiva,f.*
taste *gustar,v.*
taxi *taxi,m.*
tea *té,m.*
teaspoon *cucharilla,f; cucharita,f.*

teaspoonful	*cucharadita,f.*	thousand	*mil,n.*
technical	*técnico,m.*	three	*tres,n.*
technician	*técnico,m.*	throat	*garganta,f.*
technique	*técnica,f./adj.*	thumb	*pulgar,m.*
technologist	*tecnólogo,m.*	Thursday	*jueves,m.*
technology	*tecnología,f.*	thyroid	*tiroides,f.*
telephone	*teléfono,m.*	tie(fasten)	*atar,v*.*
tell	*decir,v*.*	tight(squeeze)	*apretado,adj.*
temperature	*temperatura,f.*	till	*hasta,adj.*
temporary	*temporero,adj.*	till	*hasta que,conj.*
ten	*diez,n.*	time	*tiempo,m.*
tender	*delicado,adj.*	time(hour)	*hora,f.*
tendon	*tendón,m.*	tip(point)	*punta,f.*
test	*examen,n.*	tired	*cansado,adj.*
testicle	*testículo,m.*	tissue	*tejido,m.*
tetanus	*tétano,m.*	to	*a; para; hasta,prep.*
than	*que,conj.*	to try	*tratar(v.) de*
thanks	*gracias*	tobacco	*tabaco,m.*
that	*ese; esa; aquel; aquella,adj.*	today	*hoy,adv.*
		toe	*dedo del pie,m.*
that	*ése; ésa; aquél; aquélla,pron.*	toenail	*uña (del dedo del pie),f.*
so that	*para que*	together	*juntamente,adv.*
that is enough	*eso basta*	toilet paper	*papel de excusado,m. papel higiénico,m.*
there	*allí; allá; ahí,adv.*		
there is/are	*hay*	tomorrow	*mañana,adv.*
thermometer	*termómetro,m.*	tongue	*lengua,f.*
thermostat	*termóstato,m.*	tonight	*esta noche; a la noche,adv.*
these	*estos; estas,adj.*		
these	*éstos; éstas,pron.*	tonsil	*amígdala,f.*
thick(not thin)	*espeso,adj.*	tonsillitis	*amigdalitis,f.*
thin(slim)	*delgado,adj.*	too	*también,adv.*
thing	*cosa,f.*	too many	*demasiados*
think	*pensar,v*.*	too much	*demasiado*
third	*tercero,adj.*	tooth	*diente,m.*
thirst	*sed,f.*	toothache	*dolor de muelas,m.*
thirsty	*sediento,adj.*	toothbrush	*cepillo de dientes,m.*
thirsty(to be)	*tener(v*.) sed*	toothpaste	*pasta dentífrica,f.*
thirteen	*trece,n.*	top of	*encima de; sobre.*
thirty	*treinta,n.*	touch	*tocar,v*.*
this	*este; esta; esto,adj.*	toupee	*peluca,f.*
this	*éste; ésta; esto,pron.*	towards	*hacia,prep.*
thoracic spine	*espina dorsal,f.*	towel	*toalla,f.*
thorax	*tórax,m.*	toxin	*toxina,f.*
those	*esos; esas; aquelos; aquellas,adj.*	toy	*juguete,m.*
		trachea	*tráquea,f.*
		traction	*tracción,f.*
those	*ésos, ésas; aquélos; aquéllas,pron.*	tranquilizer	*sedativo,m./adj.*
		tranquilize	*tranquilizar,v*.*

translate	*traducir,v*.*
translation	*traducción,f.*
translator	*traductor,m.*
transportation	*transportación,f.*
transport	*transportar,v.*
trauma	*traumatismo,m.*
travel	*viajar,v.*
tray	*bandeja,f.*
tremble	*temblar,v*.*
try	*probar,v*.*
try to	*tratar(v.) de*
tub(bath)	*bañera,f.*
tube	*tubo,m.*
tuberculosis	*tuberculosis,f.*
Tuesday	*martes,m.*
tumor	*tumor,m.*
tungsten	*tungsteno,m.*
turn	*volver(se),v*.*
turnover	*voltearse,v.*
turn over and over	*dar(v*.) repetidas vueltas*
tweezers	*pinzas,f.pl.*
twelve	*doce,n.*
twenty	*veinte,n.*
twice	*dos veces,adv.*
twin	*gemelos,m.pl./adj.*
two	*dos,n.*
type	*escribir(v*.) a máquina*
typhoid	*tifoidea,f.*
typhus	*tifus,m.*

U

ulcer	*úlcera,f.*
umbilical cord	*cordón umbilical,m.*
umbrella	*paraguas,m.*
uncle	*tío,m.*
unconscious	*inconsciente,adj.*
under	*bajo; debajo de,prep.*
under clothes	*ropa interior,f.*
undershirt	*camiseta,f.*
understand	*comprender,v.*
underwear	*ropa interior,f.*
undress	*desvestir(se),v*.*
unemployed	*desocupado,adj.*
unemployment	*desempleo,m.*
unemployment compensation	*compensación por desempleo,f.*
unfasten	*desabrochar,v.*
uniform	*uniforme,m.*
union	*unión,f.*
union(labor)	*sindicato,m.*
unless	*a menos que,conj.*
unmarried	*soltero,adj.*
unroll	*desenrollar,v.*
unsafe	*peligroso,adj.*
unsatisfactory	*no satisfactorio,adj.*
until	*hasta; hasta que,prep.*
untrue	*falso,adj.*
up	*arriba,adv.*
up to now	*hasta ahora*
upon	*en; sobre; encima de,prep.*
upper	*superior,adj.*
upright	*derecto,adj.*
upside down	*al revés; de arriba abajo*
upstairs	*arriba; en el piso de arriba,adv.*
urethra	*uretra,f.*
urgent	*urgente,adj.*
urinal	*urinario,m.*
urinate	*orinar,v.*
urine	*orina,f. (orines,m.pl.)*
use	*usar,v.*
uterus	*útero,m.*
uvula	*galillo de la garganta,m; úvula,f.*

V

vacant	*vacante,adj.*
vaccine, vaccination	*vacuna,f.*
vaccinate	*vacunar,v.*
vagina	*vagina,f.*
valve	*válvula,f.*
vein	*vena,f.*
venereal	*venéreo,adj.*
vertebral column	*columna vertebral,f.*
very	*muy,adv.*
vessel	*vasija,f.*
via	*por,prep.*

virgin *virgen,f./adj.*
vitamin *vitamina,f.*
voltage *voltaje,m.*
vomit *vomitar,v.*
vomit *vómito,m.*
vulva *vulva,f.*

W

waist *cintura,f.*
wait *esperar,v.*
waiting room *sala de espera,f.*
wake *despertar(se),v*.*
wake up *despertar(se),v*.*
walk *andar,v*; ir(v*.) a pie*
wall paréd,f.
wallet *cartera,f; monedero,m.*
want *querer,v*.*
warm *caliente; cálido , adj.*
warmth *calor,m.*
wart *verruga,*f.
wash *lavar,v.*
watch(look) *mirar,v.*
watch(wrist) *reloj de pulsera,m.*
water *agua,f.*
weak *débil,adj.*
wear *llevar,v; usar,v.*
wearing *cansado,adj.*
Wednesday *miércoles,m.*
week *semana,f.*
weekday *día de trabajo,f.*
weekend *fin de semana,m.*
weight *peso,m.*
well *bien,adv.*
what *que,pron.*
what *qué,interr.*
when *cuando,adv./conj.*
when *cuándo,interr.*
whenever *cuando; siempre que,adv./conj.*
where *donde,adv.*
where *dónde,interr.*
which *cúal; cúales,interr.*
while *mientras,conj.*
white *blanco,adj.*
who *quien; quines; que,pron.*
who *quíen; quínes; que,interr.*
why *por qué,adv.*
wide *ancho; amplio,adj.*
widow *viuda,f.*
widower *viudo,m.*
wife *esposa,f.*
wig *peluca,f.*
window *ventana,f.*
windpipe *garganta,f.*
wipe *secar,v*.*
within *dentro de,prep.*
without *sin,prep.*
woman *mujer,f.*
womb *útero,m.*
wool *lana,f.*
work(effort) *trabajo,m.*
work *trabajar,v.*
work (employment) *empleo,m.*
worse *peor; más malo,adj.*
worst *peor,adv.*
wound *herida,f.*
wrap *enrollar,v.*
wiggle *menear(se),v.*
wrist *muñeca,f.*
write *escribir,v*.*
wrong *equivocado,adj.*

X

x-ray *radiografía,f; rayo equis,m.*
x-ray room *sala de rayos equis,f.*

Y

yawn *bostezo,m.*
yawn *bostezar,v*.*
year *año,m.*
yellow *amarillo,adj.*
yes *sí,adv.*
yesterday *ayer,adv.*
young *joven,adj.*
younger *menor,adj.*

young people *gente joven,f.*

Z

zero *cero,m.*
zipcode *código postal,m; zona postal,f.*
zipper *cremallera,f; zípper,m.*